SO-BQZ-897

FRANKLIN PIERCE

1804 – 1869

Chronology – Documents – Bibliographical Aids

Edited by

IRVING J. SLOAN

Series Editor

Howard F. Bremer

Oceana Publications, Inc.
Dobbs Ferry, New York 10522
1968

Library of Congress Catalog Card Number 68-21539
Oceana Book No. 303-5

Printed in the United States of America

921
P61S

CONTENTS

EDITOR'S FOREWORD

Every attempt has been made to cite the most accurate dates in this Chronology. Diaries, documents, and similar evidence have been used to determine the exact date. If, however, later scholarship has found such dates to be obviously erroneous, the more plausible date has been used. Should this Chronology be in conflict with other authorities, the student is urged to go back to original sources as well as to such competent scholars as Roy Franklin Nichols.

This is a research tool compiled primarily for the student. While it does make some judgments on the significance of the events, it is hoped that they are reasoned judgments based on a long acquaintance with American History.

Obviously, the very selection of events by any writer is itself a judgment.

The essence of these little books is in their making available some pertinent facts and key documents **plus** a critical bibliography which should direct the student to investigate for himself additional and/or contradictory material. Documents in this volume are taken from: William MacDonald, **Select Documents of the History of the United States, 1776-1861,** and James D. Richardson, ed., **Messages and Papers of the Presidents.** Vol. 5: Pierce, 1897.

CHRONOLOGY

1804

November 23   Born, Hillsborough County, New Hampshire. Father: Benjamin. Mother: Anna Kendrick.

1814

Attended Hancock Academy and then Francestown Academy for the next six years to prepare for college entrance.

1820

September   Entered Bowdoin College in Brunswick, Maine, at the age of sixteen.

1822

Formed life-long friendship with fellow student Nathaniel Hawthorne.

1824

September 1   Graduated fifth in his class from Bowdoin (moving up from last place in the junior class ranking).

October   Returned to Hillsborough taking over his father's duties as postmaster, and studying law under the local leading lawyer, John Burnham.

1825

May   Moved to Northampton, Massachusetts, to continue legal studies under a Judge Howe.

1827

Returned to Hillsborough, completing his studies under Edmund Parker at Amherst, Hillsborough's shire town.

March   His father elected Governor of New Hampshire.

September   Admitted to practice as an attorney.

1828

January 8   Made his first public speech, an impromptu political talk on behalf of the candidacy of Andrew Jackson for president.

March   Elected moderator of town meeting in Hillsborough as a Jacksonian defeating "old guard" politicians of the community. Presided over these meetings annually for the next six years.

Father defeated in gubernatorial election.

1829

Elected as Hillsborough representative to the General Court, the New Hampshire legislature.

May   Appointed justice of the peace.

Became chairman of the committee on education in the legislature.

June   Delivered his maiden speech supporting publication of laws in state Jacksonian newspapers.

1830

Re-elected moderator and representative to the legislature.

June   Appointed chairman on towns and parishes.

1831

June   Elected Speaker of the legislature at the age of 26.

Appointed as an aid to Governor Dinsmore and thereafter became "Colonel Pierce."

1832

June   Designated with four others to form the general congressional ticket to be presented to the state electorate.

March   Elected as one of New Hampshire's five Congressmen.

August   Suffered severe bilious attack, an illness which was to plague him throughout his life.

November 28   Arrived in Washington, D.C.

December 2   Sworn in as a member of the United States House of Representatives.

Appointed member of House Judiciary Committee.

President Andrew Jackson's Annual Message dealt with the "war upon the bank" and reported removal of deposits from the national bank. This was the major issue in Congress for the next six months.

1834

February 18   Voted with the administration on the bank issue.

February 27   Delivered his first speech in House opposing a bill to grant retroactive pensions to Revolutionary veterans and their families.

November 19   Married Jane Means Appleton, daughter of the late President Jesse Appleton of Bowdoin College, in Amherst, Massachusetts.

November 29   Settled as married couple in Washington, D.C.

1835

Appointed as New Hampshire member of a select committee to investigate West Point Military Academy. His majority report condemning the institution was blocked by the minority on the committee and the report was never considered by the House.

May 27   Arrived in Hillsborough to take over new home given to newly-married couple by his father.

November   Returned to Washington without his wife whose frail health forced her to remain home.

December   Appointed by his friend, James K. Polk, Speaker of the House, to a Select Committee headed by John Quincy Adams, to deal with a boundary dispute between Ohio and Michigan.

December 18   Delivered speech opposing abolitionists' petition, describing them as "a few reckless fanatics" in his own quiet village.

1836

February 2   A son, Franklin, Jr. was born.

February 5   First son, Franklin, Jr. died.

February 8   Appointed to a Select Committee under Henry L. Pinckney of South Carolina to consider the whole question of Congressional relation to slavery. Committee reported that Congress had no power to interfere with slavery in the states, and advocated a "gag resolution" on the slavery question.

February 12   John C. Calhoun attacked a statement by Pierce about the number of abolitionists in New Hampshire as false, and produced evidence against him which appeared in a New Hampshire newspaper.

February 15   Pierce responded to charges.

Was involved in a drunken spree episode in Washington theater and remained ill for many weeks thereafter.

June 13-14   Sat in Speaker's chair during debates of bills for admission of Michigan and Arkansas.

June   Voted against rivers and harbors bill and a bill to extend Cumberland Road; always opposed spending tax money on bills which stretched constitutional interpretations and benefited particular sections of the country.

June 30   Delivered strong attack on West Point appropriations bill for maintenance; considered its activity beyond power of Congress to educate men who for most part resigned after completing education. Bill passed.

Voted in favor of resolutions to recognize new Republic of Texas as soon as possible, since it would enlarge slave area on continent.

Defeated for election in New Hampshire legislature to be United States Senator to fill vacancy created by Senator Isaac Hill's resignation to become governor.

July   Returned to Hillsborough to resume practice of law.

August   Moved household to Concord, New Hampshire.

November   New Hampshire legislature elected him United States Senator for the term beginning March 4, 1837, at age 34.

1837

February 27   Served in Chair in House while House met in Committee of the Whole on rivers and harbors bill.

March 3   Had an encounter with John Quincy Adams on a point of order; Adams was compelled to sit down.

Retired from House with record exclusively as good committee worker. No legislation or policy associated with his name.

March 4   Sworn in as Senator from New Hampshire; youngest member in the United States Senate.

May   Father partially paralyzed from stroke; mother had become senile.

September 4   Returned to Washington for special session of Congress called by Van Buren to deal with financial recession in country.

Assigned to the Committee on Manufactures.

1838

December   Mother died.

1839

April 1   Father died.

August 27   Second son, Frank Robert, born.

September   Pierce became Chairman of the Senate Pension Committee.

1840

Campaigned hard against Harrison in presidential election, considering the latter's election as a threat to return to Tory Federalism. Van Buren carried New Hampshire, but Harrison was elected.

November   Decided to resign from Senate in anticipation of the birth of another child, an event which might further weaken his wife's long-standing history of frail health; delayed decision for one year.

1841

February 16   Sent Governor Page his resignation, to take effect on the 26th.

March   Began his new personal and professional life in Concord.

April 13   Third son, Benjamin, born.

June   Became chairman of the State Central Committee of the Democratic Party.

1843

February—
March   Active speaker in political campaigns in the state.

April 29   Served as chairman of the state temperance society com-
               mittee to suppress liquor traffic in New Hampshire; he
               himself had alcoholic problem which plagued his life and
               career.

November 14   Son, Frank, died.

1844

May 14   Pierce called mass meeting in Concord inviting the "friends
               of democratic equality and religious tolerance" in response
               to riots between native Americans and the Irish in Phila-
               delphia.

June   Named state chairman of the Democratic party; Polk to be
               party candidate for president.

November   Polk carried New Hampshire in election; Pierce's cam-
               paign in the state viewed as strong factor in this victory.

December   Represented Concord in state legislature.

1845

April   Appointed by Polk district attorney for New Hampshire.

1846

August   Declined Polk's invitation to come to Washington as
               Attorney-General.

October   Declined to accept appointment to fill U.S. Senate
               vacancy.

1847

February 15   Appointed Colonel of infantry in the regular army for the
               period of the Mexican War.

March 3   Commissioned Brigadier General.

May 27   Sailed for Mexico City.

June 27   Landed in Mexico at Vera Cruz.

December 28   Arrived back in the United States after serving in Mexican
               War.

1849

November   Served as Chairman of New Hampshire Constitutional Convention to revise State Constitution. Led movement to remove bar to Catholics in public office.

1850

September   Compromise of 1850 passed by Congress.

1852

January   Delivered important address in New Boston, New Hampshire, defending his political positions.

June 1-6   Nominated for President on the 49th ballot at the National Democratic Party Convention in Baltimore, Maryland, after Stephen A. Douglas and James Buchanan "killed each other off" by the 35th ballot which was the first ballot on which Pierce's name appeared when Virginia became the first state to support him. Throughout the pre-convention campaign he remained in the background as a possible "dark horse" candidate. William Rufus De Vane King of Alabama nominated for Vice-President.

June 17-20   Whigs in Baltimore nominated Winfield Scott of New Jersey for President and William Alexander Graham of North Carolina for Vice-President.

August 11   Free Soil Party in Pittsburgh, Pennsylvania, nominated John P. Hale of New Hampshire for President, and George W. Julian of Indiana for Vice-President.

November 2   Pierce elected President with 1,601,274 votes; Scott received 1,386,580 votes; Hale won 155,285. Electoral vote was 254 for Pierce, 42 for Scott, and none for Hale.

1853

January 6   Son, Benjamin, killed in railroad accident in which both parents escaped unscathed.

TERM IN OFFICE

March 4   Inaugurated as fourteenth President of the United States on the east portico of the Capitol. Chief Justice Roger Taney administered the oath of office. His wife was not present as she was still in state of shock over recent loss of remaining son. The Inaugural Address was delivered as an oration without reference to manuscript or notes.

8 FRANKLIN PIERCE

Vice-President William R. King was sworn into office in Havana, Cuba, by special act of Congress. He was deathly ill in that city.

Members of the Cabinet were: William L. Marcy of New York, Secretary of State; James Guthrie of Kentucky, Secretary of Treasury; Jefferson Davis of Mississippi, Secretary of War; Caleb Cushing of Massachusetts, Attorney-General; James Campbell of Pennsylvania, Postmaster-General; James C. Dabbin of North Carolina, Secretary of Navy; Robert McClelland of Michigan, Secretary of Interior.

March 21 Conkling Convention signed, binding the United States and Mexico to joint protection of an American company, Sloo, in its concession of a right of way over the Isthmus of Tahuantepec.

March 22 Appointed John A. Campbell of Alabama to the United States Supreme Court.

April First diplomatic problems rose in Nicaragua over American interests in the vicinity of a "free city," Greytown, maintained by the British.

April 13 Vice-President King died before he had chance to carry out duties of his office.

May 31 Elisha K. Kane expedition departed from New York City to the Arctic.

June 21 Pierce contracted malaria.

July Commodore Matthew C. Perry sailed into the Bay of Yedo in Japan, making his demands of open ports.

July 11 Left Washington for a speech-making tour through Baltimore, Philadelphia, and New York City.

July 14 Opened Crystal Palace Exposition in New York City.

December 5 Delivered First Annual Message to Congress. Address reflected throughout his strict construction of the Constitution as well as his aim not to lead Congress but to work with it as a co-ordinate branch of government.

Further indicated his interest in territorial expansion and his dim view of abolitionists.

1854

January 4   Senator Stephen A. Douglas of Illinois introduced bill for the organization of large part of the Louisiana Purchase called the Nebraska Territory; bill's only reference to slavery called for admission of territory as state or states with or without slavery as the state constitution might prescribe.

March 31   Treaty of Kanagawa negotiated by Commander Perry opened Japanese ports to United States trade.

May 3   Vetoed "act making grant of public lands to the several states for the benefit of indigent insane persons." Dorothea Dix, leading social worker of period, played important role in drawing up bill.

May 23   Senate passed resolution calling upon President for information concerning slave situation in Cuba; Southern members alarmed at prospect of liberation of slaves there.

May 30   Signed the Kansas-Nebraska Act organizing Territories of Kansas and Nebraska and including the "popular sovereignty" principle which permitted voters to determine for themselves whether slavery will be a legalized institution at time of admission as states.

June 5   Canadian Reciprocity treaty signed with Great Britain, giving the United States offshore sea fisheries along inlets of Canada and other British possessions in area; British were granted fishing privileges along United States shores to 36th parallel.

June 29   Appointed Andrew H. Reeder of Pennsylvania as first governor of the Kansas Territory.

June 30   Gadsden Purchase treaty ratified; negotiated by James Gadsden of South Carolina, Minister to Mexico, whereby the United States paid $10,000,000 for some 45,000 square miles of land between the Rio Grande and the Colorado Rivers.

July 22   Signed agreement with Russia "recognizing that free ships make free goods except contraband and that neutral property on board belligerent vessels is not confiscable.''

July 31 Sent message to Senate on the seizure of American steamer, *Black Warrior,* by Spanish authorities in Cuba, on technical violation of port rules.

October 18 Ostend Manifesto dispatched by three American envoys who met in Belgium: James Buchanan, Minister to England; Pierre Soule, Minister to Spain; James Mason, Minister to France. Document declared that the United States ought to purchase Cuba, concluding that "we should be justified in wrestling it from Spain if we possess the power." While Pierce Administration repudiated the declaration, it left a legacy of problems in the conduct of foreign relations both for Pierce and his successors, but at the same time enhanced Buchanan's presidential aspirations by gathering Southern support.

December 4 Delivered Second Annual Message, most of which was devoted to foreign affairs in the background of the Crimean War then going on in Europe.

1855
January 1 Mrs. Pierce made her Washington debut at New Year's Ball in the White House.

February Appointed Augustus C. Dodge of Iowa as Minister to Spain to replace Pierre Soulé.

February 17 Vetoed the French spoliation bill "to provide for the ascertainment of claims of American citizens for spoliations committed by the French prior to the 31st of July, 1801."

March 3 Vetoed internal improvements bill providing for deepening channel over the St. Clair's flats and in St. Mary's River in Michigan. This reflected his opposition to Federal action in the states.

Congress approved Administration measure providing for a registered mail system and the requirement of postage stamps to be affixed to all mail.

April Portrait painted by Francis B. Carpenter, leading American artist of era.

June 9   Instructed James Buchanan, Minister to Great Britain, to call upon British Foreign Office to account for British recruiting of Americans to serve in British army in the war against Russia in violation of United States neutrality acts.

July 28   Dismissed Governor Reeder of Kansas Territory for his involvement in fraudulent land sales.

August 1   Appointed Townsend Harris of New York as United States Consul General in Japan.

                Appointed Wilson Shannon of Ohio as Governor of Kansas Territory.

November 14   New Hampshire Democratic Convention instructed its delegates to national convention in 1856 to vote for Pierce's renomination, thereby throwing the President's hat into the ring.

December 8   Issued a proclamation against the invasion of Nicaragua by the military adventurer, William Walker, who was backed by U.S. commercial interests.

December 31   Third Annual Message sent to Congress late because House of Representatives failed to organize all through the month. Out of patience in a rare example of firm leadership on his part, he sent message at end of month in any case. Relations with Great Britain and the issue of slavery in the Territories dominated the message.

1856

January 24   In Special Message to Congress, asked for law to provide for inhabitants of Kansas to hold a constitutional convention to frame a constitution for admission to Union as a state.

February 11   Issued Proclamation calling for end of violence on part of citizens "both of adjoining and of distant states, to abstain from unauthorized intermeddling in the local concerns of the Kansas Territory."

May 14   Received emissary from William Walker and thereby unofficially recognized latter's seizure of Nicaragua which opened up that country to slavery.

May 19   Vetoed internal improvements bills to improve mouth of Mississippi River and to deepen channel over the flats of St. Mary's River in Michigan.

May 21   Lawrence, Kansas, sacked and captured by pro-slavery forces, inflaming Northern anti-slavery sentiment.

May 22   Senator Charles Sumner of Massachusetts was brutally assaulted on the floor of the Senate by Representative Preston S. Brooks of South Carolina in retaliation for Sumner's speech on "The Crime Against Kansas," which included an attack on Brooks' uncle, Senator Andrew P. Butler of South Carolina.

May 25   John Brown carried out the Pottawatomie Creek massacre, executing five proslavery colonists at midnight.

June 2-6   Having disappointed his supporters in the South in not going far enough to support extension of slavery, and aroused enmity in the North for going too far to protect this institution, the Democratic party failed to renominate him at its national convention in Cincinnati, Ohio. He was behind Buchanan on every ballot from the 1st to the 17th which finally placed the latter in nomination.

June 2   Issued Proclamation confirming boundary lines between Mexico and United States as established in treaty of December 3, 1853.

June 19   Republican party nominated John C. Fremont of California as its candidate for President.

July 28   Removed Governor Shannon of Kansas Territory and appointed John W. Geary of Pennsylvania in his place.

August 11   Vetoed bill to improve De Moines Rapid in Mississippi River.

August 14   Vetoed bills for the improvement of the Palapsco River "and to render the port of Baltimore accessible to the war steamers of the United States."

August 18   Congress adjourned without passing an army appropriations bill, leaving inadequate troops to cope with difficulties in Kansas, Washington Territory and California.

August 28   In Special Session called by Pierce, Congress passed army bill.

Congress passed five internal improvements bills over Presidential vetoes of May 19, August 11 and August 14.

September   Visited New Hampshire and was honored at a number of receptions and mass meetings. Purpose of trip was to assure victory in state for Democratic candidate for President.

October 17   Treaty signed with Great Britain which resolved disputes in Nicaragua and Costa Rica.

November 4   Buchanan elected President, but failed to carry New Hampshire.

December 2   Fourth Annual Message reviewed his achievements briefly and focused largely on the threat to the Union of Republican views on the slavery issue.

1857

January 1   Held an "open house" in the White House for the public.

February 27   Last Friday evening "levee" at which officials in Washington came to bid farewell to the retiring President.

February   Refused French suggestion of armed co-operation in forcing China to make more liberal concessions to Western powers.

March 3   Final meeting of Cabinet held.

Signed bills granting government aids to the development of the Atlantic cable, for overland mail service to the Pacific, and the construction of five sloops of war for the navy.

March 4   No carriage appeared to take him to meet Buchanan for the Inaugural parade so he ordered his own and met the President-elect at the Willard Hotel.

RETIREMENT

May 1	William Walker surrendered to United States naval commander after having been ousted as President of Nicaragua under influence of Cornelius Vanderbilt who now controlled commercial interests there.
June 1	Made his first public appearance since the Inauguration at a banquet in Andover, Massachusetts, where he warned New England to preserve the Union and the Constitution by respecting rights of Southern states to maintain their institutions.
November	Set sail for trip to island of Madeira.

1858
Spent the year with wife traveling through Europe.

1859

August	Returned to the United States, and purchased property in Concord, New Hampshire, on which to build new permanent home.
October 16	Deplored John Brown's raid at Harpers Ferry Arsenal as being "in violation of all law, human and divine."

1860

January 6	Dispatched letter to Jefferson Davis expressing his belief that Davis would be best presidential candidate in forthcoming election.
January 7	Departed from NewYork for five month stay in Nassau.
June	Arrived in New York from southern tour; again pressed to seek nomination, he declined.
	Awarded honorary LLD. from Dartmouth College.
November 4	Abraham Lincoln elected president on the Republican ticket.
December 24-25	Was urged by John A. Campbell of Alabama, whom he had appointed to the Supreme Court, to serve as Commissioner to Alabama "peace convention" which each of the Southern states were holding. He declined because of

health, but proposed that the South be allowed six months to work out a peaceful settlement with the North. Nothing came of plan.

April 12-14 Civil War began with firing upon and surrender of Fort Sumter.

April 16 Wrote Van Buren proposing that he call ex-Presidents to Philadelphia to issue appeal to country for peaceful settlement; no record of response.

1861

August Made three week visit to the West.

December 24 Received official letter from Secretary of State William H. Seward, enclosing copy of anonymous communication charging Pierce with disloyalty to the Union in connection with his activities on his recent Western trip.

1862

March Newspapers published letter and charges after Seward had accepted Pierce's denial. Although finally proved to be a hoax, the impression on the public mind remained that he was disloyal.

1863

January 1 Emancipation Proclamation issued by Lincoln; Pierce condemned document as attempt to "butcher" the white race for the sake of "inflicting" freedom on Negroes who were incapable of benefiting from it.

Spent much of the year agitating against Lincoln and the conduct of the war.

July 4 Delivered strong attack on the idea of maintaining the Union by force in a speech in Capital Square, Concord. His public reputation was almost ruined after this address.

December 2 Wife died.

1864

May 19 Nathaniel Hawthorne, his oldest friend, died in Plymouth, New Hampshire, while the two were traveling together in the White Mountains; Pierce was excluded as pallbearer at funeral because of hostility toward him.

1865

April 15   Mob attacked his house in Concord when no flag appeared to be displayed in mourning of Lincoln's assassination.

December 3   Baptized in St. Paul's Episcopal Church.

1866

Spent most of his time at Little Boar's Head on the New Hampshire coast.

1869

September   Became ill and returned to Concord.

October 8   Died in his home in Concord and was buried in Old North Cemetery, Concord, New Hampshire. Period of national mourning declared by President U.S. Grant.

DOCUMENTS

INAUGURAL ADDRESS
March 4, 1853

When Chief Justice Roger Taney administered the oath to Pierce, he raised his right hand and broke with tradition by affirming rather than swearing. The new President then delivered his carefully prepared address without a manuscript or notes. The grief referred to in the first sentence of his speech was the tragic death of his young son in January. Mrs. Pierce was still in such a state that she did not come to Washington until several months after the inauguration. The address itself anticipated much of the policy of the new administration. Continental expansion, strict construction of the Constitution, and upholding the right of slave states to maintain their institutional system of slavery, were the issues which prevailed for the duration of his presidency.

My Countrymen:

It is a relief to feel that no heart but my own can know the personal regret and bitter sorrow over which I have been borne to a position so suitable for others rather than desirable for myself.

The circumstances under which I have been called for a limited period to preside over the destinies of the Republic fill me with a profound sense of responsibility, but with nothing like shrinking apprehension. I repair to the post assigned me not as to one sought, but in obedience to the unsolicited expression of your will, answerable only for a fearless, faithful, and diligent exercise of my best powers. I ought to be, and am, truly grateful for the rare manifestation of the nation's confidence; but this, so far from lightening my obligations, only adds to their weight. You have summoned me in my weakness; you must sustain me by your strength. When looking for the fulfillment of reasonable requirements, you will not be unmindful of the great changes which have occurred, even within the last quarter of a century, and the consequent augmentation and complexity of duties imposed in the administration both of your home and foreign affairs.

Whether the elements of inherent force in the Republic have kept pace with its unparalleled progression in territory, population, and wealth has been the subject of earnest thought and discussion on both sides of the ocean. Less than sixty-four years ago the Father of his Country made "the" then "recent accession of the important State of North Carolina to the Constitution of the United States" one of the subjects of his special congratulation. At that moment, however, when the agitation consequent upon the Revolutionary struggle had hardly subsided, when we were just emerging from the weakness and embarrassments of the Confederation, there was an evident consciousness of vigor equal to the great mission so wisely and bravely fulfilled by our fathers. It was not a presumptuous assurance, but a calm faith, springing from a clear view of the sources of power in a government constituted like ours. It is no paradox to say that although comparatively weak the new-born nation was intrinsically strong. Inconsiderable in population and apparent resources, it was upheld by a broad and intelligent comprehension of rights and an all-pervading purpose to maintain them, stronger than armaments. It came from the furnace of the Revolution, tempered to the necessities of the times. The thoughts of the men of that day were as practical as their sentiments were patriotic. They wasted no portion of their energies upon idle and delusive speculations, but with a firm and fearless step advanced beyond the governmental landmarks which had hitherto circumscribed the limits of human freedom and planted their standard, where it has stood against dangers which have threatened from abroad, and internal agitation, which has at times fearfully menaced at home. They proved themselves equal to the solution of the great problem, to understand which their minds had been illuminated by the dawning lights of the Revolution. The object sought was not a thing dreamed of; it was a thing realized. They had exhibited not only the power to achieve, but, what all history affirms to be so much more unusual, the capacity to maintain. The oppressed throughout the world from that day to the present have turned their eyes hitherward, not to find those lights extinguished or to fear lest they should wane, but to be constantly cheered by their steady and increasing radiance.

In this our country has, in my judgment, thus far fulfilled its highest duty to suffering humanity. It has spoken and will continue to speak, not only by its words, but by its acts, the language of sympathy, encouragement, and hope to those who earnestly listen to tones which pronounce for the largest rational liberty. But after all, the most animating encouragement and potent appeal for freedom will be its own history—its trials and its triumphs. Preeminently, the powers of our advocacy reposes in our example; but no example, be it remembered, can be powerful for lasting good, whatever apparent advantages may be gained, which is not based upon eternal principles of right and justice. Our fathers decided for themselves both upon the hour to declare and the hour to strike. They were their own judges of the circumstances under which it became them to pledge to each other "their lives, their fortunes, and their sacred honor" for the acquisition of the priceless inheritance transmitted to us. The energy with which that great conflict was opened and, under the guidance of a manifest and beneficient Providence the uncomplaining endurance with which it was prosecuted to its consummation were only surpassed by the wisdom and patriotic spirit of concession which characterized all the counsels of the early fathers.

One of the most impressive evidences of that wisdom is to be found in the fact that the actual working of our system has dispelled a degree of solicitude which at the outset disturbed bold hearts and far-reaching intellects. The apprehension of dangers from extended territory, multiplied States, accumulated wealth, and augmented population has proved to be unfounded. The stars upon your banner have become nearly threefold their original number; your densely populated possessions skirt the shores of the two great oceans; and yet this vast increase of people and territory has not only shown itself compatible with the harmonious action of the States and Federal Government in their respective constitutional spheres, but has afforded an additional guaranty of the strength and integrity of both.

With an experience thus suggestive and cheering, the policy of my Administration will not be controlled by any timid forebodings of evil from expansion. Indeed, it is not to be disguised that our attitude as a nation and our position on the globe render the acquisition of certain possessions not within our jurisdiction eminently important for our protection, if not in the future essential for the preservation of the rights of commerce and the peace of the world. Should they be obtained, it will be through no grasping spirit, but with a view to obvious national interest and security, and in a manner entirely consistent with the strictest observance of national faith. We have nothing in our history or position to invite aggression; we have everything to beckon us to the cultivation of relations of peace and amity with all nations. Purposes, therefore, at once just and pacific will be significantly marked in the conduct of our foreign affairs. I intend that my Administration shall leave no blot upon our fair record, and trust I may safely give the assurance that no act within the legitimate scope of my constitutional control will be tolerated on the part of any portion of our citizens which can not challenge a ready justification before the tribunal of the civilized world. An Administration would be unworthy of confidence at home or respect abroad should it cease to be influenced by the conviction that no apparent advantage can be purchased at a price so dear as that of national wrong or dishonor. It is not your privilege as a nation to speak of a distant past. The striking incidents of your history, replete with instruction and furnishing abundant grounds for hopeful confidence, are comprised in a period comparatively brief. But if your past is limited, your future is boundless. Its obligations throng the unexplored pathway of advancement, and will be limitless as duration. Hence a sound and comprehensive policy should embrace not less the distant future than the urgent present.

The great objects of our pursuit as a people are best to be attained by peace, and are entirely consistent with the tranquillity and interests of the rest of mankind. With the neighboring nations upon our continent we should cultivate kindly and fraternal relations. We can desire nothing in regard to them so much as to see them consolidate their strength and pursue the paths of prosperity and happiness. If in the course of their growth we should open new channels of trade and create additional facilities for friendly intercourse, the benefits realized will be equal and mutual. Of the complicated European systems of national policy we have heretofore been independent. From their wars, their tumults, and anxieties we have been, happily, almost entirely exempt. Whilst these are confined to the nations which gave them existence, and within their legitimate jurisdiction, they can not affect us except as they appeal to our sympathies in the cause of human freedom and universal advancement. But the vast interests of commerce are common to all mankind, and the advantages of trade and international intercourse must always present a noble field for the moral influence of a great people.

With these views firmly and honestly carried out, we have a right to expect, and shall under all circumstances require, prompt reciprocity. The rights which belong to us as a nation are not alone to be regarded, but those which pertain to every citizen in his individual capacity, at home and abroad, must be sacredly maintained. So long as he can discern every star in its place upon that ensign, without wealth to purchase for him preferment or title to secure for him place, it will be his privilege, and must be his acknowledged right, to stand unabashed even in the presence of princes, with a proud consciousness that he is himself one of a nation of sovereigns and that he can not in legitimate pursuit wander so far from home that the agent whom he shall leave behind in the place which I now occupy will not see that no rude hand of power or tyrannical passion is laid upon him with impunity. He must realize that upon every sea and on every soil where our enterprise may rightfully seek the protection of our flag American citizenship is an inviolable panoply for the security of American rights. And in this connection it can hardly be necessary to reaffirm a principle which should now be regarded as fundamental. The rights, security, and repose of this Confederacy reject the idea of interference or colonization on this side of the ocean by any foreign power beyond present jurisdiction as utterly inadmissible.

The opportunities of observation furnished by my brief experience as a soldier confirmed in my own mind the opinion, entertained and acted upon by others from the formation of the Government, that the main-

tenance of large standing armies in our country would be not only dangerous, but unnecessary. They also illustrated the importance—I might well
say the absolute necessity—of the military science and practical skill furnished in such an eminent degree by the institution which has made your
Army what it is, under the discipline and instruction of officers not more
distinguished for their solid attainments, gallantry, and devotion to the
public service than for unobtrusive bearing and high moral tone. The
Army as organized must be the nucleus around which in every time of
need the strength of your military power, the sure bulwark of your defense—a national militia—may be readily formed into a well-disciplined and
efficient organization. And the skill and self-devotion of the Navy assure
you that you may take the performance of the past as a pledge for the
future, and may confidently expect that the flag which has waved its un-
tarnished folds over every sea will still float in undiminished honor. But
these, like many other subjects, will be appropriately brought at a future
time to the attention of the coordinate branches of the Government, to
which I shall always look with profound respect and with trustful confidence that they will accord to me the aid and support which I shall so
much need and which their experience and wisdom will readily suggest.

In the administration of domestic affairs you expect a devoted integrity
in the public service and an observance of rigid economy in all departments, so marked as never justly to be questioned. If this reasonable ex-
pectation be not realized, I frankly confess that one of your leading
hopes is doomed to disappointment, and that my efforts in a very important particular must result in a humiliating failure. Offices can be
properly regarded only in the light of aids for the accomplishment of
these objects, and as occupancy can confer no prerogative nor importunate
desire for preferment any claim, the public interest imperatively demands
that they be considered with sole reference to the duties to be performed.
Good citizens may well claim the protection of good laws and the benign
influence of good government, but a claim for office is what the people
of a republic should never recognize. No reasonable man of any party
will expect the Administration to be so regardless of its responsibility and
of the obvious elements of success as to retain persons known to be under
the influence of political hostility and partisan prejudice in positions
which will require not only severe labor, but cordial cooperation. Having
no implied engagements to ratify, no rewards to bestow, no resentments
to remember, and no personal wishes to consult in selections for official
station, I shall fulfill this difficult and delicate trust, admitting no motive
as worthy either of my character or position which does not contemplate
an efficient discharge of duty and the best interests of my country. I
acknowledge my obligations to the masses of my countrymen, and to
them alone. Higher objects than personal aggrandizement gave direction
and energy to their exertions in the late canvass, and they shall not be

disappointed. They require at my hands diligence, integrity, and capacity wherever there are duties to be performed. Without these qualities in their public servants, more stringent laws for the prevention or punishment of fraud, negligence, and speculation will be vain. With them they will be unnecessary.

But these are not the only points to which you look for vigilant watchfulness. The dangers of a concentration of all power in the general government of a confederacy so vast as ours are too obvious to be disregarded. You have a right, therefore, to expect your agents in every department to regard strictly the limits imposed upon them by the Constitution of the United States. The great scheme of our constitutional liberty rests upon a proper distribution of power between the State and Federal authorities, and experience has shown that the harmony and happiness of our people must depend upon a just discrimination between the separate rights and responsibilities of the States and your common rights and obligations under the General Government; and here, in my opinion, are the considerations which should form the true basis of future concord in regard to the questions which most seriously disturbed public tranquillity. If the Federal Government will confine itself to the exercise of powers clearly granted by the Constitution, it can hardly happen that its action upon any question should endanger the institutions of the States or interfere with their right to manage matters strictly domestic according to the will of their own people.

In expressing briefly my views upon an important subject which has recently agitated the nation to almost a fearful degree, I am moved by no other impulse than a most earnest desire for the perpetuation of that Union which has made us what we are, showering upon us blessings and conferring a power and influence which our fathers could hardly have anticipated, even with their most sanguine hopes directed to a far-off future. The sentiments I now announce were not unknown before the expression of the voice which called me here. My own position upon this subject was clear and unequivocal, upon the record of my words and my acts, and it is only recurred to at this time because silence might perhaps be misconstrued. With the Union my best and dearest earthly hopes are entwined. Without it what are we individually or collectively? What becomes of the noblest field ever opened for the advancement of our race in religion, in government, in the arts, and in all that dignifies and adorns mankind? From that radiant constellation which both illumines our own way and points out to struggling nations their course, let but a single star be lost, and if these be not utter darkness, the luster of the whole is dimmed. Do my countrymen need any assurance that such a catastrophe is not to overtake them while I possess the power to stay it? It is with me an earnest and vital belief that as the Union has been the source, under Providence, of our prosperity to this time, so it is the surest pledge of a continuance of the blessings we have enjoyed, and which we are sacredly bound to transmit undiminished to our children. The field of calm and free discussion in our country is open, and will always be so, but never has been and never can be traversed for good in a spirit of sectionalism and uncharitableness. The founders of the Republic dealt with things as they were presented to them, in a spirit of self-sacrificing patriotism, and, as time has proved, with a comprehensive wisdom which it will always be safe for us to consult. Every measure tending to strengthen the fraternal feelings of all the members of our Union has had my heartfelt approbation. To every theory of society or government, whether the offspring of feverish ambition or of morbid enthusiasm, calculated to dissolve the bonds of law and affection which unite us, I shall interpose a ready and stern resistance. I believe that involuntary servitude, as it exists in different States of this Confederacy, is recognized by the Constitution. I believe that it stands like any other admitted right, and that the States where it exists are entitled to efficient remedies to enforce the constitutional provisions. I hold that the laws of 1850, commonly called the "compromise measures," are strictly constitutional and to be unhesitatingly carried into effect. I believe that the constituted authorities of this Republic are bound to regard the rights of the South in this respect as they would view any other legal and constitutional right, and that the laws to enforce them should be respected and obeyed, not with a reluctance encouraged by abstract opinions as to their propriety in a different state of society, but cheerfully and according to the decisions of the tribunal to which their exposition belongs. Such have been, and are, my convictions, and upon them I shall act. I fervently hope that the question is at rest, and that no sectional or ambitious or fanatical excitement may again threaten the durability of our institutions or obscure the light of our prosperity.

But let not the foundation of our hope rest upon man's wisdom. It will not be sufficient that sectional prejudices find no place in the public deliberations. It will not be sufficient that the rash counsels of human passion are rejected. It must be felt that there is no national security but in the nation's humble, acknowledged dependence upon God and his overruling providence.

We have been carried in safety through a perilous crisis. Wise counsels, like those which gave us the Constitution, prevailed to uphold it. Let the period be remembered as an admonition, and not as an encouragement, in any section of the Union, to make experiments where experiments are fraught with such fearful hazard. Let it be impressed upon all hearts that, beautiful as our fabric is, no earthly power or wisdom could ever reunite its broken fragments. Standing, as I do, almost within view of the green slopes of Monticello, and, as it were, within reach of the tomb of Washington, with all the cherished memories of the past gathering around me like so many eloquent voices of exhortation from heaven, I can express no better hope for my country that that the kind Providence which smiled upon our fathers may enable their children to preserve the blessings they have inherited.

FRANKLIN PIERCE

FIRST ANNUAL MESSAGE
December 5, 1853

In his first Message, Pierce set the tone of his entire administration. It contained an air of deference to the judgment of Congress; he was not going to lead. The three major issues he dealt with here were expansion, a railroad to the Pacific, and the relations of the sections with reference to slavery. He also stated his belief in strictly adhering to the Constitution. Finally, he outlined a laissez-faire policy for the Federal government.

WASHINGTON, D.C., December 5, 1853

Fellow-Citizens of the Senate and of the House of Representatives:

The interest with which the people of the Republic anticipate the assembling of Congress and the fulfillment on that occasion of the duty imposed upon a new President is one of the best evidences of their capacity to realize the hopes of the founders of a political system at once complex and symmetrical. While the different branches of the Government are to a certain extent independent of each other, the duties of all alike have direct reference to the source of power. Fortunately, under this system no man is so high and none so humble in the scale of public station as to escape from the scrutiny or to be exempt from the responsibility which all official functions imply.

Upon the justice and intelligence of the masses, in a government thus organized, is the sole reliance of the confederacy and the only security for honest and earnest devotion to its interests against the usurpations and encroachments of power on the one hand and the assaults of personal ambition on the other.

The interest of which I have spoken is inseparable from an inquiring, self-governing community, but stimulated, doubtless, at the present time by the unsettled condition of our relations with several foreign powers, by the new obligations resulting from a sudden extension of the field of enterprise, by the spirit with which that field has been entered and the amazing energy with which its resources for meeting the demands of humanity have been developed. . . .

Our diplomatic relations with foreign powers have undergone no essential change since the adjournment of the last Congress. With some of them questions of a disturbing character are still pending, but there are good reasons to believe that these may all be amicably adjusted.

For some years past Great Britain has so construed the first article of the convention of the 20th of April, 1818, in regard to the fisheries on the northeastern coast, as to exclude our citizens from some of the fishing grounds to which they freely resorted for nearly a quarter of a century subsequent to the date of that treaty. The United States have never acquiesced in this construction, but have always claimed for their fishermen all the rights which they had so long enjoyed without molestation. With a view to remove all difficulties on the subject, to extend the rights of our fishermen beyond the limits fixed by the convention of 1818, and to regulate trade between the United States and the British North American Provinces, a negotiation has been opened with a fair prospect of a favorable result. To protect our fishermen in the enjoyment of their rights and prevent collision between them and British fishermen, I deemed it expedient to station a naval force in that quarter during the fishing season.

Embarrassing questions have also arisen between the two Governments in regard to Central America. Great Britain has proposed to settle them by an amicable arrangement, and our minister at London is instructed to enter into negotiations on that subject. . . .

It is in many respects desirable that the boundary line between the United States and the British Provinces in the northwest, as designated in the convention of the 15th of June, 1846, and especially that part which separates the Territory of Washington from the British possessions on the north, should be traced and marked. I therefore present the subject to your notice.

With France our relations continue on the most friendly footing. The extensive commerce between the United States and that country might, it is conceived, be released from some unnecessary restrictions to the mutual advantage of both parties. With a view to this object, some progress has been made in negotiating a treaty of commerce and navigation.

Independently of our valuable trade with Spain, we have important political relations with her growing out of our neighborhood to the islands of Cuba and Puerto Rico. I am happy to announce that since the last Congress no attempts have been made by unauthorized expedition within the United States against either of those colonies. Should any movement be manifested within our limits, all the means at my command will be vigorously exerted to repress it. Several annoying occurrences have taken place at Havana, or in the vicinity of the island of Cuba, between our citizens and the Spanish authorities. Considering the proximity of that island to our shores, lying, as it does, in the track of trade between some of our principal cities, and the suspicious vigilance with which foreign intercourse, particularly that with the United States, is there guarded, a repetition of such occurrences may well be apprehended. . . .

The condition of China at this time renders it probable that some important changes will occur in that vast Empire which will lead to a more unrestricted intercourse with it. The commissioner to that country who has been recently appointed is instructed to avail himself of all occasions to open and extend our commercial relations, not only with the Empire of China, but with other Asiatic nations.

In 1852 an expedition was sent to Japan, under the command of Commodore Perry, for the purpose of opening commercial intercourse with that Empire. Intelligence has been received of his arrival there and of his having made known to the Emperor of Japan the object of his visit. But it is not yet ascertained how far the Emperor will be disposed to abandon his restrictive policy and open that populous country to a commercial intercourse with the United States.

It has been my earnest desire to maintain friendly intercourse with the Governments upon this continent and to aid them in preserving good understanding among themselves. With Mexico a dispute has arisen as to the true boundary line between our Territory of New Mexico and the Mexican State of Chihuahua. A former commissioner of the United States, employed in running that line pursuant to the treaty of Guadalupe Hidalgo, made a serious mistake in determining the initial point on the Rio Grande; but inasmuch as his decision was clearly a departure from the directions for tracing the boundary contained in that treaty, and was not concurred in by the surveyor appointed on the part of the United States, whose concurrence was necessary to give validity to that decision, this Government is not concluded thereby; but that of Mexico takes a different view of the subject.

There are also other questions of considerable magnitude pending between the two Republics. Our minister in Mexico has ample instructions to adjust them. Negotiations have been opened, but sufficient progress has not been made therein to enable me to speak of the probable result. Impressed with the importance of maintaining amicable relations with that Republic and of yielding with liberality to all her just claims, it is reasonable to expect that an arrangement mutually satisfactory to both countries may be concluded and a lasting friendship between confirmed and perpetuated.

Congress having provided for a full mission to the States of Central America, a minister was sent thither in July last. As yet he has had time to visit only one of these States (Nicaragua), where he was received in the most friendly manner. It is hoped that his presence and good offices will have a benign effect in composing the dissensions which prevail among them, and in establishing still more intimate and friendly relations between them respectively and between each of them and the United States. . . .

We are thus not only at peace with all foreign countries, but, in regard to political affairs, are exempt from any cause of serious disquietude in our domestic relations.

The controversies which have agitated the country heretofore are passing away with the causes which produced them and the passions which they had awakened; or, if any trace of them remains, it may be reasonably hoped that it will only be perceived in the zealous rivalry of all good citizens to testify their respect for the rights of the States, their devotion to the Union, and their common determination that each one of the States, its institutions, its welfare, and its domestic peace, shall be held alike secure under the sacred aegis of the Constitution. . . .

The United States have continued gradually and steadily to expand through acquisitions of territory, which, how much soever some of them may have been questioned, are now universally seen and admitted to have been wise in policy, just in character, and a great element in the advancement of our country, and with it of the human race, in freedom, in prosperity, and in happiness. The thirteen States have grown to be thirty-one, with relations reaching to Europe on the one side and on the other to the distant realms of Asia.

I am deeply sensible of the immense responsibility which the present magnitude of the Republic and the diversity and multiplicity of its interests devolves upon me, the alleviation of which so far as relates to the immediate conduct of the public business, is, first, in my reliance on the wisdom and patriotism of the two Houses of Congress, and, secondly, in the directions afforded me by the principles of public polity affirmed by our fathers of the epoch of 1798, sanctioned by long experience, and consecrated anew by the overwhelming voice of the people of the United States.

Recurring to these principles, which constitute the organic basis of union, we perceive that vast as are the functions and the duties of the Federal Government, vested in or intrusted to its three great departments—the legislative, executive, and judicial—yet the substantive power, the popular force, and the large capacities for social and material development exist in the respective States, which, all being of themselves well-constituted republics, as they preceded so they alone are capable of maintaining and perpetuating the American Union. The Federal Government has its appropriate line of action in the specific and limited powers conferred on it by the Constitution, chiefly as to those things in which the States have a common interest in their relations to one another and to foreign governments, while the great mass of interests which belong to cultivated men—the ordinary business of life, the springs of industry, all the diversified personal and domestic affairs of society—rest securely upon the general reserved powers of the people of the several States. There is the effective democracy of the nation, and there the vital essence of its being and its greatness.

Of the practical consequences which flow from the nature of the Federal Government, the primary one is the duty of administering with integrity and fidelity the high trust reposed in it by the Constitution, especially in the application of the public funds as drawn by taxation from the people and appropriated to specific objects by Congress.

Happily, I have no occasion to suggest any radical changes in the financial policy of the Government. Ours is almost, if not absolutely, the solitary power of Christendom having a surplus revenue drawn immediately from imposts on commerce, and therefore measured by the spontaneous enterprise and national prosperity of the country, with such indirect relation to agriculture, manufactures, and the products of the earth and sea as to violate no constitutional doctrine and yet vigorously promote the general welfare. Neither as to the sources of the public treasure nor as to the manner of keeping and managing it does any grave controversy now prevail, there being a general acquiescence in the wisdom of the present system.

The report of the Secretary of the Treasury will exhibit in detail the state of the public finances and the condition of the various branches of the public service administered by that Department of the Government.

The revenue of the country, levied almost insensibly to the taxpayer, goes on from year to year, increasing beyond either the interests or the prospective wants of the Government.

This fact of increasing surplus in the Treasury became the subject of anxious consideration at a very early period of my Administration, and the path of duty in regard to it seemed to me obvious and clear, namely: First, to apply the surplus revenue to the discharge of the public debt so far as it could judiciously be done, and, secondly, to devise means for the gradual reduction of the revenue to the standards of the public exigencies. . . .

Among the objects meriting your attention will be important recommendations from the Secretaries of War and Navy. I am fully satisfied that the Navy of the United States is not in a condition of strength and efficiency commensurate with the magnitude of our commercial and other interests, and commend to your especial attention the suggestions on this subject made by the Secretary of the Navy. I respectfully submit that the Army, which under our system must always be regarded with the highest interest as a nucleus around which the volunteer forces of the nation gather in the hour of danger, requires augmentation, or modification, to adapt it to the present extended limits and frontier relations of the country and the condition of the Indian tribes in the interior of the continent, the necessity of which will appear in the communications of the Secretaries of War and the Interior. . . .

Regarding our public domain as chiefly valuable to provide homes for the industrious and enterprising, I am not prepared to recommend any essential change in the land system, except by modifications in favor of the actual settler and an extension of the preemption principle in certain cases, for reasons and on grounds which will be fully developed in the reports to be laid before you.

Congress, representing the proprietors of the territorial domain and charged especially with power to dispose of territory belonging to the United States, has for a long course of years, beginning with the Administration of Mr. Jefferson, exercised the power to construct roads within the Territories, and there are so many and obvious distinctions between this exercise of power and that of making roads within the States that the former has never been considered subject to such objections as apply to the latter; and such may now be considered the settled construction of the power of the Federal Government upon the subject.

Numerous applications have been and no doubt will continue to be made for grants of land in aid of the construction of railways. It is not believed to be within the intent and meaning of the Constitution that the power to dispose of the public domain should be used otherwise than might be expected from a prudent proprietor, and therefore that grants of land to aid in the construction of roads should be restricted to cases where it would be for the interest of a proprietor under like circumstances thus to contribute to the construction of these works. For the practical operation of such grants thus far in advancing the interests of the States in which the works are located, and at the same time the substantial interests of all the other States, by enhancing the value and promoting the rapid sale of the public domain. I refer you to the report of the Secretary of the Interior. A careful examination, however, will show that this experience is the result of a just discrimination and will be far from affording encouragement to a reckless or indiscriminate extension of the principle. . . .

The subject of internal improvements, claiming alike the interest and good will of all, has nevertheless, been the basis of much political discussion and has stood as a deep-graven line of division between statesmen of eminent ability and patriotism. The rule of strict construction of all powers delegated by the States to the General Government has arrayed itself from time to time against the rapid progress of expenditures from the National Treasury on works of a local character within the States. Memorable as an epoch in the history of this subject is the message of President Jackson of the 27th of May, 1830, which met the system of internal improvements in its comparative infancy; but so rapid had been its growth that the projected appropriations in that year for works of this character had risen to the alarming amount of more than $100,000,000.

In that message the President admitted the difficulty of bringing back the operations of the Government to the construction of the Constitution set up in 1798, and marked it as an admonitory proof of the necessity of guarding that instrument with sleepless vigilance against the authority of precedents which had not the sanction of its most plainly defined powers.

Our Government exists under a written compact between sovereign

States, uniting for specific objects and with specific grants to their general agent. If, then, in the progress of its administration there have been departures from the terms and intent of the compact, it is and will ever be proper to refer back to the fixed standard which our fathers left us and to make a stern effort to conform our action to it. It would seem that the fact of a principle having been resisted from the first by many of the wisest and most patriotic men of the Republic, and a policy having provoked constant strife without arriving at a conclusion which can be regarded as satisfactory to its most earnest advocates, should suggest the inquiry whether there may not be a plan likely to be crowned by happier results. Without perceiving any sound distinction or intending to assert any principle as opposed to improvements needed for the protection of internal commerce which does not equally apply to improvements upon the seaboard for the protection of foreign commerce, I submit to you whether it may not be safely anticipated that if the policy were once settled against appropriations by the General Government for local improvements for the benefit of commerce, localities requiring expenditures would not, by modes and means clearly legitimate and proper, raise the fund necessary for such constructions as the safety or other interests of their commerce might require.

If that can be regarded as a system which in the experience of more than thirty years has at no time so commanded the public judgment as to give it the character of a settled policy; which, though it has produced some works of conceded importance, has been attended with an expenditure quite disproportionate to their value and has resulted in squandering large sums upon objects which have answered no valuable purpose, the interests of all the States require it to be abandoned unless hopes may be indulged for the future which find no warrant in the past.

With an anxious desire for the completion of the works which are regarded by all good citizens with sincere interest, I have deemed it my duty to ask at your hands a deliberate reconsideration of the question, with a hope that, animated by a desire to promote the permanent and substantial interests of the country, your wisdom may prove equal to the task of devising and maturing a plan which, applied to this subject, may promise something better than constant strife, the suspension of the powers of local enterprise, the exciting of vain hopes, and the disappointment of cherished expectations.

In expending the appropriations made by the last Congress several cases have arisen in relation to works for the improvement of harbors which involve questions as to the right of soil and jurisdiction, and have threatened conflict between the authority of the State and General Governments. The right to construct a breakwater, jetty, or dam would seem necessarily to carry with it the power to protect and preserve such constructions. This can only be effectually done by having jurisdiction over the soil. But no clause of the Constitution is found on which to rest the claim of the United States to exercise jurisdiction over the soil of a State except that conferred by the eighth section of the first article of the Constitution. It is, then, submitted whether, in all cases where constructions are to be erected by the General Government, the right of soil should not first be obtained and legislative provision be made to cover all such cases. . . .

There is one subject of a domestic nature which, from its intrinsic importance and the many interesting questions of future policy which it involves, can not fail to receive your early attention. I allude to the means of communication by which different parts of the wide expanse of our country are to be placed in closer connection for purposes both of defense and commercial intercourse, and more especially such as appertain to the communication of those great divisions of the Union which lie on the opposite sides of the Rocky Mountains.

That the Government has not been unmindful of this heretofore is apparent from the aid it has afforded through appropriations for mail facilities and other purposes. But the general subject will now present itself under aspects more imposing and more purely national by reason of the surveys ordered by Congress, and now in the process of completion, for communication by railway across the continent, and wholly within the limits of the United States.

The power to declare war, to raise and support armies, to provide and maintain a navy, and to call forth the militia to execute the laws, suppress insurrections, and repel invasions was conferred upon Congress as means to provide for the common defense and to protect a territory and a population now widespread and vastly multiplied. As incidental to and indispensable for the exercise of this power, it must sometimes be necessary to construct military roads and protect harbors of refuge. To appropriations by Congress for such objects no sound objection can be raised. Happily for our country, its peaceful policy and rapidly increasing population impose upon us no urgent necessity for preparation, and leave but few trackless deserts between assailable points and a patriotic people every ready and generally able to protect them. These necessary links the enterprise and energy of our people are steadily and boldly struggling to supply. All experience affirms that wherever private enterprise will avail it is most wise for the General Government to leave to that and individual watchfulness the location and execution of all means of communication. . . .

The magnitude of the enterprise contemplated has aroused and will doubtless continue to excite a very general interest throughout the country. In its political, its commercial, and its military bearings it has varied great, and increasing claims to consideration. The heavy expense, the great delay, and, at times, fatality attending travel by either of the Isthmus routes have demonstrated the advantage which would result from interterritorial communication by such safe and rapid means as a railroad would supply.

These difficulties, which have been encountered in a period of peace, would be magnified and still further increased in time of war. But whilst the embarrassments already encountered and others under new contingencies to be anticipated may serve strikingly to exhibit the importance of such a work, neither these nor all considerations combined can have an appreciable value when weighed against the obligation strictly to adhere to the Constitution and faithfully to execute the powers it confers.

Within this limit and to the extent of the interest of the Government involved it would seem both expedient and proper if an economical and practicable route shall be found to aid by all constitutional means in the construction of a road which will unite by speedy transit the populations of the Pacific and Atlantic States. To guard against misconception, it should be remarked that although the power to construct or aid in the construction of a road within the limits of a Territory is not embarrassed by that question of jurisdiction which would arise within the limits of a State, it is, nevertheless, held to be of doubtful power and more than doubtful propriety, even within the limits of a Territory, for the General Government to undertake to administer the affairs of a railroad, a canal, or other similar construction, and therefore that its connection with a work of this character should be incidental rather than primary. I will only add at present that, fully appreciating the magnitude of the subject and solicitous that the Atlantic and Pacific shores of the Republic may be bound together by inseparable ties of common interest, as well as of common fealty and attachment to the Union, I shall be disposed, so far as my own action is concerned, to follow the lights of the Constitution as expounded and illustrated by those whose opinions and expositions constitute the standard of my political faith in regard to the powers of the Federal Government. It is, I trust, not necessary to say that no grandeur of enterprise and no present urgent inducement promising popular favor will lead me to disregard those lights or to depart from that path which experience has proved to be safe, and which is now radiant with the glow of prosperity and legitimate constitutional progress. We can afford to wait, but we can not afford to overlook the ark of our security.

It is no part of my purpose to give prominence to any subject which may properly be regarded as set at rest by the deliberate judgment of the people. But while the present is bright with promise and the future full of demand and inducement for the exercise of active intelligence, the past can never be without useful lessons of admonition and instruction. If its dangers serve not as beacons, they will evidently fail to fulfill the object of a wise design. When the grave shall have closed over all who are now endeavoring to meet the obligations of duty, the year 1850 will be recurred to as a period filled with anxious apprehension. A successful war had just terminated. Peace brought with it a vast augmentation of territory. Disturbing questions arose bearing upon the domestic institutions of one portion of the Confederacy and involving the constitutional rights of the States. But notwithstanding differences of opinion and sentiment which then existed in relation to details and specific provisions, the acquiescence of distinguished citizens, whose devotion to the Union can never be doubted, has given renewed vigor to our institutions and restored a sense of repose and security to the public mind throughout the Confederacy. That this repose is to suffer no shock during my official term, if I have power to avert it, those who placed me here may be assured. The wisdom of men who knew what independence cost, who had put all at stake upon the issue of the Revolutionary struggle, disposed of the subject to which I refer in the only way consistent with the Union of these States and with the march of power and prosperity which has made us what we are. It is a significant fact that from the adoption of the Constitution until the officers and soldiers of the Revolution had passed to their graves, or, through the infirmities of age and wounds, had ceased to participate actively in public affairs, there was not merely a quiet acquiescence in, but a prompt vindication of, the constitutional rights of the States. The reserved powers were scrupulously respected. No statesman put forth the narrow views of casuists to justify interference and agitation, but the spirit of the compact was regarded as sacred in the eye of honor and indispensable for the great experiment of civil liberty, which, environed by inherent difficulties, was yet borne forward in apparent weakness by a power superior to all obstacles. There is no condemnation which the voice of freedom will not pronounce upon us should we prove faithless to this great trust. While men inhabiting different parts of this vast continent can no more be expected to hold the same opinions or entertain the same sentiments than every variety of climate or soil can be expected to furnish the same agricultural products, they can unite in a common object and sustain common principles essential to the maintenance of that object. The gallant men of the South and the North could stand together during the struggle of the Revolution; they could stand together in the more trying period which succeeded the clangor of arms. As their united valor was adequate to all the trials of the camp and dangers of the field, so their united wisdom proved equal to the greater task of founding upon a deep and broad basis institutions which it has been our privilege to enjoy and will ever be our most sacred duty to sustain. It is but the feeble expression of a faith strong and universal to say that their sons, whose blood mingled so often upon the same field during the War of 1812 and who have more recently borne in triumph the flag of the country upon a foreign soil, will never permit alienation of feeling to weaken the power of their united efforts nor internal dissensions to paralyze the great arm of freedom, uplifted for the vindication of self-government. . . .

The growth of our population has now brought us, in the destined career of our national history, to a point at which it well behooves us to expand our vision over the vast prospective.

The successive decennial returns of the census since the adoption of the

Constitution have revealed a law of steady, progressive development, which may be stated in general terms as a duplication every quarter century. Carried forward from the point already reached for only a short period of time, as applicable to the existence of a nation, this law of progress, if unchecked, will bring us to almost incredible results. A large allowance for a diminished proportional effect of emigration would not very materially reduce the estimate, while the increased average duration of human life known to have already resulted from the scientific and hygienic improvements of the past fifty years will tend to keep up through the next fifty, or perhaps hundred, the same ratio of growth which has been thus revealed in our past progress; and to the influence of these causes may be added the influx of laboring masses from eastern Asia to the Pacific side of our possessions, together with the probable accession of the populations already existing in other parts of our hemisphere, which within the period in question will feel with yearly increasing force the natural attraction of so vast, powerful, and prosperous a confederation of self-governing republics and will seek the privilege of being admitted within its safe and happy bosom, transferring with themselves, by a peaceful and healthy process of incorporation, spacious regions of virgin and exuberant soil, which are destined to swarm with the fast-growing and fast-spreading millions of our race.

These considerations seem fully to justify the presumption that the law of population above stated will continue to act with undiminished effect through at least the next half century, and that thousands of persons who have already arrived at maturity and are now exercising the rights of freemen will close their eyes on the spectacle of more than 100,000,000 of population embraced within the majestic proportions of the American Union. It is not merely as an interesting topic of speculation that I present these views for your consideration. They have important practical bearings upon all the political duties we are called upon to perform. Heretofore our system of government has worked on what may be termed a miniature scale in comparison with the development which it must thus assume within a future so near at hand as scarcely to be beyond the present of the existing generation.

It is evident that a confederation so vast and so varied, both in numbers and in territorial extent, in habits and in interests, could only be kept in national cohesion by the strictest fidelity to the principles of the Constitution as understood by those who have adhered to the most restricted construction of the powers granted by the people and the States. Interpreted and applied according to those principles, the great compact adapts itself with healthy ease and freedom to an unlimited extension of that benign system of federative self-government of which it is our glorious and, I trust, immortal charter. Let us, then, with redoubled vigilance, be on our guard against yielding to the temptation of the exercise of doubtful powers, even under the pressure of the motives of conceded temporary advantage and apparent temporary expediency.

The minimum of Federal government compatible with the maintenance of national unity and efficient action in our relations with the rest of the world should afford the rule and measure of construction of our powers under the general clauses of the Constitution. A spirit of strict deference to the sovereign rights and dignity of every State, rather than a disposition to subordinate the States into a provincial relation to the central authority should characterize all our exercise of the respective powers temporarily vested in us as a sacred trust from the generous confidence of our constitutents.

In like manner, as a manifestly indispensable condition of the perpetuation of the Union and of the realization of that magnificent national future adverted to, does the duty become yearly stronger and clearer upon us, as citizens of the several States, to cultivate a fraternal and affectionate spirit, language, and conduct in regard to other States and in relation to the varied interests, institutions, and habits of sentiment and opinion which may respectively characterize them. Mutual forbearance, respect, and noninterference in our personal action as citizens and an enlarged exercise of the most liberal principles of comity in the public dealings of State with State, whether in legislation or in the execution of laws, are the means to perpetuate that confidence and fraternity the decay of which a mere political union, on so vast a scale, could not long survive.

In still another point of view is an important practical duty suggested by this consideration of the magnitude of dimensions to which our political system, with its corresponding machinery of government, is so rapidly expanding. With increased vigilance does it require us to cultivate the cardinal virtues of public frugality and official integrity and purity. Public affairs ought to be so conducted that a settled conviction shall pervade the entire Union that nothing short of the highest tone and standard of public morality marks every part of the administration and legislation of the General Government. Thus will the federal system, whatever expansion time and progress may give it, continue more and more deeply rooted in the love and confidence of the people. . . .

Entertaining unlimited confidence in your intelligent and patriotic devotion to the public interest, and being conscious of no motives on my part which are not inseparable from the honor and advancement of my country, I hope it may be my privilege to deserve and secure not only your cordial cooperation in great public measures, but also those relations of mutual confidence and regard which it is always so desirable to cultivate between members of coordinate branches of the Government.

Franklin Pierce

SPECIAL REPORT ON THE "BLACK WARRIOR" AFFAIR
March 15, 1854

In February, 1854, Spanish authorities at Havana seized the American steamer, "Black Warrior," for a technical violation of custom regulations. Southerners and southern sympathizers anxious to add Cuba for the expansion of slavery, called for breaking relations, if not war, with Spain. Pierre Soule, United States minister to Spain, represented the American claim and would have created a break with Spain were it not for the tactful diplomacy of Secretary of State William Marcy which resulted in Spain's release of the ship with an apology and payment of damages. Nevertheless, pressure for the annexation of Cuba increased and it remained a burning issue throughout the years of Pierce's tenure.

WASHINGTON, March 5, 1854.

To the House of Representatives:

In compliance with the resolution of the House of Representatives of the 10th instant, I herewith transmit a report of the Secretary of State, containing all the information received at the Department in relation to the seizure of the *Black Warrior* at Havanna on the 28th ultimo.

There have been in the course of a few years past many other instances of aggression upon our commerce, violations of the rights of American citizens, and insults to the national flag by the Spanish authorities in Cuba, and all attempts to obtain redress have led to protracted, and as yet fruitless, negotiations.

The documents in these cases are voluminous, and when prepared will be sent to Congress.

Those now transmitted relate exclusively to the seizure of the *Black Warrior,* and present so clear a case of wrong that it would be reasonable to expect full indemnity therefor as soon as this unjustifiable and offensive conduct shall be made known to Her Catholic Majesty's Government; but similar expectations in other cases have not been realized.

The offending party is at our doors with large powers for aggression, but none, it is alleged, for reparation. The source of redress is in another hemisphere, and the answers to our just complaints made to the home Government are but the repetition of excuses rendered by inferior officials to their superiors in reply to representations of misconduct. The peculiar situation of the parties has undoubtedly much aggravated the annoyances and injuries which our citizens have suffered from the Cuban authorities, and Spain does not seem to appreciate to its full extent her responsibility for the conduct of these authorities. In giving very extraordinary powers to them she owes it to justice and to her friendly relations with this Government to guard with great vigilance against the exorbitant exercise of these powers, and in case of injuries to provide for prompt redress.

I have already taken measures to present to the Government of Spain the wanton injury of the Cuban authorities in the detention and seizure of the **Black Warrior,** and to demand immediate indemnity for the injury which has thereby resulted to our citizens.

In view of the position of the island of Cuba, its proximity to our coast, the relations which it must ever bear to our commercial and other interests, it is vain to expect that a series of unfriendly acts infringing our commercial rights and the adoption of a policy threatening the honor and security of these States can long consist with peaceful relations.

In case the measures taken for amicable adjustment of our difficulties with Spain should, unfortunately, fail, I shall not hestitate to use the authority and means which Congress may grant to insure the observance of our just rights, to obtain redress for injuries received, and to vindicate the honor of our flag.

In anticipation of that contingency, which I earnestly hope may not arise, I suggest to Congress the propriety of adopting such provisional measures as the exigency may seem to demand.

FRANKLIN PIERCE

SECOND ANNUAL MESSAGE
December 4, 1854.

Disaster had been frequent in the past year and the setting of the President's Message was in a background of the Crimean War, the crop shortage, epidemic, financial panic, shipwreck and political disintegration in connection with the slavery issue. The chief purpose of the Message was to restate the administration's foreign policy, and the bulk of it was devoted to that subject. The reports of his cabinet members concerning their respective departments were quickly summarized. Pierce discussed his efforts to secure the adoption of the principle that "free ships make free goods." Finally, he prided himself in keeping the United States out of entangling alliances in spite of the war in Europe.

WASHINGTON, *December 4, 1854.*

Fellow-Citizens of the Senate and of the House of Representatives:

The past has been an eventful year, and will be hereafter referred to as a marked epoch in the history of the world. While we have been happily preserved from the calamities of war, our domestic prosperity has not been entirely uninterrupted. The crops in portions of the country have been nearly cut off. Disease has prevailed to a greater extent than usual, and the sacrifice of human life through casualties by sea and land is without parallel. But the pestilence has swept by, and restored salubrity invites the absent to their homes and the return of business to its ordinary channels. If the earth has rewarded the labor of the husbandman less bountifully than in preceding seasons, it has left him with abundance for domestic wants and a large surplus for exportation. In the present, therefore, as in the past, we find ample grounds for reverent thankfulness to the God of grace and providence for His protecting care and merciful dealings with us as a people.

Although our attention has been arrested by painful interest in passing events, yet our country feels no more than the slight vibrations of the convulsions which have shaken Europe. As individuals we can not repress sympathy with human suffering nor regret for the causes which produce it; as a nation we are reminded that whatever interrupts the peace or checks the prosperity of any part of Christendom tends more or less to involve our own. The condition of States is not unlike that of individuals; they are mutually dependent upon each other. Amicable relations between them and reciprocal good will are essential for the promotion of whatever is desirable in their moral, social, and political course of action and our geographical position, so remote from Europe, increasing disposition has been manifested by some of its Governments to supervise and in certain respects to direct our foreign policy. In plans for adjusting the balance of power among themselves they have assumed to take us into account, and would constrain us to conform our conduct to their views. One or another of the powers of Europe has from time to time undertaken to enforce arbitrary regulations contrary in many respects to established principles of international law. That law the United States have in their foreign intercourse uniformly respected and observed, and they can not recognize any such interpolations therein as the temporary interests of others may suggest. They do not admit that the sovereigns of one continent or of a particular community of states can legislate for all others.

Leaving the transatlantic nations to adjust their political system in the way they may think best for their common welfare, the independent powers of this continent may well assert the right to be exempt from all annoying interference on their part. Systematic abstinence from intimate political connection with distant foreign nations does not conflict with giving the widest range to our foreign commerce. This distinction, so clearly marked in history, seems to have been overlooked or disregarded by some leading foreign states. Our refusal to be brought within and subjected to their peculiar system has, I fear, created a jealous distrust of our conduct and induced on their part occasional acts of disturbing effect upon our foreign relations. Our present attitude and past course give assurances, which should not be questioned, that our purposes are not aggressive nor threatening to the safety and welfare of other nations. Our military establishment in time of peace is adapted to maintain exterior defenses and to preserve order among the aboriginal tribes within the limits of the Union. Our naval force is intended only for the protection of our citizens abroad and of our commerce, diffused, as it is, over all the seas of the globe. The Government of the United States, being essentially pacific in policy, stands prepared to repel invasion by the voluntary service of a patriotic people, and provides no permanent means of foreign aggression. These considerations should allay all apprehension that we are disposed to encroach on the rights or endanger the security of other states.

Some European powers have regarded with disquieting concern the territorial expansion of the United States. This rapid growth has resulted from the legitimate exercise of sovereign rights belonging alike to all nations, and by many liberally exercised. Under such circumstances it could hardly have been expected that those among them which have within a comparatively recent period subdued and absorbed ancient kingdoms, planted their standards on every continent, and now possess or claim the control of the islands of every ocean as their appropriate domain would look with unfriendly sentiments upon the acquisitions of this country, in every instance honorably obtained, or would feel themselves justified in imputing our advancement to a spirit of aggression or to a passion for political predominance.

Our foreign commerce has reached a magnitude and extent nearly equal to that of the first maritime power of the earth, and exceeding that of any other. Over this great interest, in which not only our merchants, but all classes of citizens, at least indirectly, are concerned, it is the duty of the executive and legislative branches of the Government to exercise a careful supervision and adopt proper measures for its protection. The policy which I had in view in regard to this interest embraces its future as well as its present security. Long experience has shown that, in general, when the principal powers of Europe are engaged in war the rights of neutral nations are endangered. This consideration led, in the progress of the War of our Independence, to the formation of the celebrated confederacy of armed neutrality, a primary object of which was to assert the doctrine that free ships make free goods, except in the case of articles contraband of war—a doctrine which from the very commencement of our national being has been a cherished idea of the statesmen of this country. At one period or another every maritime power has by some solemn treaty stipulation recognized that principle, and it might have been hoped that it would come to be universally received and respected as a rule of international law. But the refusal of one power prevented this, and in the next great war which ensued—that of the French Revolution—it failed to be respected among the belligerent States of Europe. Notwithstanding this, the principle is generally admitted to be a sound and salutary one, so much so that at the commencement of the existing war in Europe Great Britain and France announced their purpose to observe it for the present; not, however, as a recognized international right, but as a mere concession for the time being. The cooperation, however, of these two powerful maritime nations in the interest of neutral rights appeared to me to afford an occasion inviting and justifying on the part of the United States a renewed effort to make the doctrine in question a principle of international law, by means of special conventions between the several powers of Europe and America. Accordingly, a proposition embracing not only the rule that free ships make free goods, except contraband articles, but also the less contested one that neutral property other than contraband, though on board enemy's ships, shall be exempt from confiscation, has been submitted by this Government to those of Europe and America
. . . .

Since the adjournment of Congress the ratifications of the treaty between the United States and Great Britain relative to coast fisheries and to reciprocal trade with the British North American Provinces have been exchanged, and some of its anticipated advantages are already enjoyed by us, although its full execution was to abide certain acts of legislation not yet fully performed. So soon as it was ratified Great Britain opened to our commerce the free navigation of the river St. Lawrence and to our fishermen unmolested access to the shores and bays, from which they had been previously excluded, on the coasts of her North American

Provinces; in return for which she asked for the introduction free of duty into the ports of the United States of the fish caught on the same coast by British fishermen. This being the compensation stipulated in the treaty for privileges of the highest importance and value to the United States, which were thus voluntarily yielded before it became effective, the request seemed to me to be a reasonable one; but it could not be acceded to from want of authority to suspend our laws imposing duties upon all foreign fish. . . .

There is difference of opinion between the United States and Great Britain as to the boundary line of the Territory of Washington adjoining the British possessions on the Pacific, which has already led to difficulties on the part of the citizens and local authorities of the two Governments. I recommend that provision be made for a commission, to be joined by one on the part of Her Britannic Majesty, for the purpose of running and establishing the line in controversy. Certain stipulations of the third and fourth articles of the treaty concluded by the United States and Great Britain in 1846, regarding possessory rights of the Hudsons Bay Company and property of the Pugets Sound Agricultural Company, have given rise to serious disputes, and it is important to all concerned that summary means of settling them amicably should be devised. I have reason to believe that an arrangement can be made on just terms for the extinguishment of the rights in question, embracing also the right of the Hudsons Bay Company to the navigation of the river Columbia; and I therefore suggest to your consideration the expediency of making a contingent appropriation for that purpose. . . .

The position of our affairs with Spain remains as at the close of the last session. Internal agitation, assuming very nearly the character of political revolution, has recently convulsed that country. The late ministers were violently expelled from power, and men of very different views in relation to its internal affairs have succeeded. Since this change there has been no propitious opportunity to resume and press on negotiations for the adjustment of serious questions of difficulty between the Spanish Government and the United States. There is reason to believe that our minister will find the present Government more favorably inclined than the preceding to comply with our just demands and to make suitable arrangements for restoring harmony and preserving peace between the two countries. . . .

The naval expedition dispatched about two years since for the purpose of establishing relations with the Empire of Japan has been ably and skillfully conducted to a successful termination by the officer to whom it was intrusted. A treaty opening certain of the ports of that populous country has been negotiated, and in order to give full effect thereto it only remains to exchange ratifications and adopt requisite commercial regulations.

The treaty lately concluded between the United States and Mexico settled some of our most embarrassing difficulties with that country, but numerous claims upon it for wrongs and injuries to our citizens remained unadjusted, and many new cases have been recently added to the former list of grievances. Our legation has been earnest in its endeavors to obtain from the Mexican Government a favorable consideration of these claims, but hitherto without success. This failure is probably in some measure to be ascribed to the disturbed condition of that country. It has been my anxious desire to maintain friendly relations with the Mexican Republic and to cause its rights and territories to be respected, not only by our citizens, but by foreigners who have resorted to the United States for the purpose of organizing hostile expeditions against some of the States of that Republic. The defenseless condition in which its frontiers have been left has stimulated lawless adventurers to embark in these enterprises and greatly increased the difficulty of enforcing our obligations of neutrality. Regarding it as my solemn duty to fulfill efficiently these obligations, not only toward Mexico, but other foreign nations, I have exerted all the powers with which I am invested to defeat such proceedings and bring to punishment those who by taking a part therein violated our laws. The energy and activity of our civil and military authorities have frustrated the designs of those who meditated expeditions of this character except in two instances. One of these, composed of foreigners, was at first countenanced and aided by the Mexican Government itself, it having been deceived as to their real object. The other, small in number, eluded the vigilance of the magistrates at San Francisco and succeeded in reaching the Mexican territories; but the effective measures taken by this Government compelled the abandonment of the undertaking.

The commission to establish the new line between the United States and Mexico, according to the provisions of the treaty of the 30th of December last, has been organized, and the work is already commenced. . . .

Convenient means of transit between the several parts of a country are not only desirable for the objects of commercial and personal communication, but essential to its existence under one government. Separated, as are the Atlantic and Pacific coasts of the United States, by the whole breadth of the continent, still the inhabitants of each are closely bound together by community of origin and institutions and by strong attachment to the Union. Hence the constant and increasing intercourse and vast interchange of commercial productions between these remote divisions of the Republic. At the present time the most practicable and only commodious routes for communication between them are by the way of the isthmus of Central America. It is the duty of the Government to secure these avenues against all danger of interruption.

In relation to Central America, perplexing questions existed between the United States and Great Britain at the time of the cession of California. These, as well as questions which subsequently arose concerning interoceanic communication across the Isthmus, were, as it was supposed, adjusted by the treaty of April 19, 1850, but, unfortunately, they have been reopened by serious misunderstanding as to the import of some of its provisions, a readjustment of which is now under consideration. Our minister at London has made strenuous efforts to accomplish this desirable object, but has not yet found it possible to bring the negotiations to a termination. . . .

Passing from foreign to domestic affairs, your attention is naturally directed to the financial condition of the country, always a subject of general interest. For complete and exact information regarding the finances and the various branches of the public service connected therewith I refer you to the report of the Secretary of the Treasury, from which it will appear that the amount of revenue during the last fiscal year from all sources was $73,549,705, and that the public expenditures for the same period, exclusive of payments on account of the public debt, amounted to $51,018,249. . . .

This statement exhibits the fact that the annual income of the Government greatly exceeds the amount of its public debt, which latter remains unpaid only because the time of payment has not yet matured, and it can not be discharged at once except at the option of public creditors, who prefer to retain the securities of the United States; and the other fact, not less striking, that the annual revenue from all sources exceeds by many millions of dollars the amount needed for a prudent and economical administration of the Government. . . .

The experience of the last year furnishes additional reasons, I regret to say, of a painful character, for the recommendation heretofore made to provide for increasing the military force employed in the Territory inhabited by the Indians. The settlers on the frontier have suffered much from the incursions of predatory bands, and large parties of emigrants to our Pacific possessions have been massacred with impunity. The recurrence of such scenes can only be prevented by teaching these wild tribes the power of and their responsibility to the United States. From the garrisons of our frontier posts it is only possible to detach troops in small bodies; and though these have on all occasions displayed a gallantry and a stern devotion to duty which on a larger field would have commanded universal admiration, they have usually suffered severely in these conflicts with superior numbers, and have sometimes been entirely sacrificed. All the disposable force of the Army is already employed on this service, and is known to be wholly inadequate to the protection which should be afforded. The public mind of the country has been recently shocked by savage atrocities committed upon defenseless emigrants and border settlements, and hardly less by the unnecessary destruction of valuable lives where inadequate detachments of troops have undertaken to furnish the needed aid. Without increase of the military force these scenes will be repeated, it is to be feared, on a larger scale and with more disastrous consequences. Congress, I am sure, will perceive that the plainest duties and responsibilities of Government are involved in this question, and I doubt not that prompt action may be confidently anticipated when delay must be attended by such fearful hazards. . . .

The valuable services constantly rendered by the Army and its inestimable importance as the nucleus around which the volunteer forces of the nation can promptly gather in the hour of danger, sufficiently attest the wisdom of maintaining a military peace establishment; but the theory of our system and the wise practice under it require that any proposed augmentation in time of peace be only commensurate with our extended limits and frontier relations. While scrupulously adhering to this principle, I find in existing circumstances a necessity for increase of our military force, and it is believed that four new regiments, two of infantry and two of mounted men, will be sufficient to meet the present exigency. If it were necessary carefully to weigh the cost in a case of such urgency, it would be shown that the additional expense would be comparatively light. . . .

The suggestions which I submitted in my annual message of last year in reference to grants of land in aid of the construction of railways were less full and explicit than the magnitude of the subject and subsequent developments would seem to render proper and desirable. Of the soundness of the principle then asserted with regard to the limitation of the power of Congress I entertain no doubt, but in its application it is not enough that the value of lands in a particular locality may be enhanced; that, in fact, a larger amount of money may probably be received in a given time for alternate sections than could have been realized for all the sections without the impulse and influence of the proposed improvements. A prudent proprietor looks beyond limited sections of his domain, beyond present results to the ultimate effect which a particular line of policy is likely to produce upon all his possessions and interests. The Government, which is trustee in this matter for the people of the States, is bound to take the same wise and comprehensive view. Prior to and during the last session of Congress upward of 30,000,000 acres of land were withdrawn from public sale with a view to applications for grants of this character pending before Congress. A careful review of the whole subject led me to direct that all such orders be abrogated and the lands restored to market, and instructions were immediately given to that effect. The applications at the last session contemplated the construction of more than 5,000 miles of road and grants to the amount of nearly 20,000,000 acres of the public domain. Even admitting the right on the part of Congress to be unquestionable, is it quite clear that the proposed grants would be productive of good, and not evil? The different projects are confined for the present to eleven States of this Union and one Territory. The reasons assigned for the grants show that it is proposed to put the works speedily in process of construction. When we reflect that since the commencement of the construction of railways in the United States, stimulated, as they have been, by the large dividends realized from the earlier works over the great thoroughfares and between the most important points of commerce and population, encouraged by State legislation, and pressed forward by the amazing energy of private enterprise, only 17,000 miles have been completed in all the States in a quarter of a century; when we see the crippled condition of many works commenced and prosecuted upon what were deemed to be sound principles and safe calculations; when we contemplate the enormous absorption of capital withdrawn from the ordinary channels of business, the extravagant rates of interest at this moment paid to continue operations, the bankruptcies, not merely in money but in character, and the inevitable effect upon finances generally, can it be doubted that the tendency is to run to excess in this matter? Is it wise to augment this excess by encouraging hopes of sudden wealth expected to flow from magnificent schemes dependent upon the action of Congress? Does the spirit which has produced such results need to be stimulated or checked? Is it not the better rule to leave all these works to private enterprise, regulated and, when expedient, aided by the cooperation of States? If constructed by private capital the stimulant and the check go together and furnish a salutary restraint against speculative schemes and extravagance. But it is manifest that with the most effective guards there is danger of going too fast and too far.

We may well pause before a proposition contemplating a simultaneous movement for the construction of railroads which in extent will equal, exclusive of the great Pacific road and all its branches, nearly one-third of the entire length of such works now completed in the United States, and which can not cost with equipments less than $150,000,000. The dangers likely to result from combinations of interests of this character can hardly be overestimated. But independently of these considerations, where is the accurate knowledge, the comprehensive intelligence, which shall discriminate between the relative claims of these twenty-eight proposed roads in eleven States and one Territory? Where will you begin and where end? If to enable these companies to execute their proposed works it is necessary that the aid of the General Government be primarily given, the policy will present a problem so comprehensive in its bearings and so important to our political and social well-being as to claim in anticipation the severest analysis. Entertaining these views, I recur with satisfaction to the experience and action of the last session of Congress as furnishing assurance that the subject will not fail to elicit a careful reexamination and rigid scrutiny.

It was my intention to present on this occasion some suggestions regarding internal improvements by the General Government, which want of time at the close of the last session prevented my submitting on the return to the House of Representatives with objections of the bill entitled "An act making appropriations for the repair, preservation, and completion of certain public works heretofore commenced under the authority of law;" but the space in this communication already occupied with other matter of immediate public exigency constrains me to reserve that subject for a special message, which will be transmitted to the two Houses of Congress at an early day. . . .

My former recommendations in relation to suitable provision for various objects of deep interest to the inhabitants of the District of Columbia are renewed. Many of these objects partake largely of a national character, and are important independently of their relation to the prosperity of the only considerable organized community in the Union entirely unrepresented in Congress. . . .

Our forefathers of the thirteen united colonies, in acquiring their independence and in founding this Republic of the United States of America, have devolved upon us, their descendants, the greatest and the most noble trust ever committed to the hands of man, imposing upon all, and especially such as the public will may have invested for the time being with political functions, the most sacred obligations. We have to maintain inviolate the great doctrine of the inherent right of popular self-government; to reconcile the largest liberty of the individual citizen with complete security of the public order; to render cheerful obedience to the laws of the land, to unite in enforcing their execution, and to frown indignantly on all combinations to resist them; to harmonize a sincere and ardent devotion to the institutions of religious faith with the most universal religious toleration; to preserve the rights of all by causing each to respect those of the other; to carry forward every social improvement to the uttermost limit of human perfectibility, by the free action of mind upon mind, not by the obtrusive intervention of misapplied force; to uphold the integrity and guard the limitations of our organic law; to preserve sacred from all touch of usurpation, as the very palladium of our political salvation, the reserved rights and powers of the several States and of the people; to cherish with loyal fealty and devoted affection this Union, as the only sure foundation on which the hopes of civil liberty rest; to administer government with vigilant integrity and rigid economy; to cultivate peace and friendship with foreign nations, and to demand and exact equal justice from all, but to do wrong to none; to eschew intermeddling with the national policy and the domestic repose of other governments, and to repel it from our own; never to shrink from war when the rights and the honor of the country call us to arms, but to cultivate in preference the arts of peace, seek enlargement of the rights of neutrality, and elevate and liberalize the intercourse of nations; and by such just and honorable means, and such only, whilst exalting the condition of the Republic, to assure to it the legitimate influence and the benign authority of a great example amongst all the powers of Christendom.

Under the solemnity of these convictions the blessing of Almighty God is earnestly invoked to attend upon your deliberations and upon all the counsels and acts of the Government, to the end that, with common zeal and common efforts, we may, in humble submission to the divine will, cooperate for the promotion of the supreme good of these United States.

FRANKLIN PIERCE

VETO OF INTERNAL IMPROVEMENTS PROGRAM
December 30, 1854

As a strict constructionist of the Constitution, Pierce very naturally took a limited view of federal spenkng very naturally took a limited view of federal spending on internal improvements within the states. This message was essentially the official Democratic party statement on the rivers and harbors question. It argued that the federal government had powers which could could be applied to rivers and harbors for military and naval purposes, yet the question which "of the infinite variety of possible river and harbor improvements, are within the scope of the power delegated by the constitution" still remained unsettled. Feeling that any concessions on internal improvement appropriations would let loose a flood of such measures, he laid down as a policy the conditions which should govern any such legislation.

WASHINGTON, *December 30, 1854.*

To the Senate and House of Representatives:

In returning to the House of Representatives, in which it originated, a bill entitled "An act making appropriations for the repair, preservation, and completion of certain public works heretofore commenced under the authority of law," it became necessary for me, owing to the late day at which the bill was passed, to state my objections to it very briefly, announcing at the same time a purpose to resume the subject for more deliberate discussion at the present session of Congress; for, while by no means insensible of the arduousness of the task thus undertaken by me, I conceived that the two Houses were entitled to an exposition of the considerations which had induced dissent on my part from their conclusions in this instance.

The great constitutional question of the power of the General Government in relation to internal improvements has been the subject of earnest difference of opinion at every period of the history of the United States. Annual and special messages of successive Presidents have been occupied with it, sometimes in remarks on the general topic and frequently in objection to particular bills. The conflicting sentiments of eminent statesmen, expressed in Congress or in conventions called expressly to devise, if possible, some plan calculated to relieve the subject of the embarrassments with which it is environed, while they have directed public attention strongly to the magnitude of the interests involved, have yet left unsettled the limits, not merely of expediency, but of constitutional power, in relation to works of this class by the General Government.

What is intended by the phrase "internal improvements"? What does it embrace and what exclude? No such language is found in the Constitution. Not only is it not an expression of ascertainable constitutional power, but it has no sufficient exactness of meaning to be of any value as the basis of a safe conclusion either of constitutional law or of practical statesmanship.

President John Quincy Adams, in claiming on one occasion, after his retirement from office, the authorship of the idea of introducing into the administration of the affairs of the General Government, "a permanent and regular system" of internal improvements, speaks of it as a system by which "the whole Union would have been checkered over with railroads and canals," affording "high wages and constant employment to hundreds of thousands of laborers;" and he places it in express contrast with the construction of such works by the legislation of the States and by private enterprise.

It is quite obvious that if there be any constitutional power which authorizes the construction of "railroads and canals" by Congress, the same power must comprehend turnpikes and ordinary carriage roads; nay, it must extend to the construction of bridges, to the draining of marshes, to the erection of levees, to the construction of canals of irrigation; in a word, to all the possible means of the material improvement of the earth, by developing its natural resources anywhere and everywhere, even within the proper jurisdiction of the several States. But if there be any constitutional power thus comprehensive in its nature, must not the same power embrace within its scope other kinds of improvement of equal utility in themselves and equally important to the welfare of the whole country? President Jefferson, while intimating the expediency of so amending the Constitution as to comprise objects of physical progress and well-being, does not fail to perceive that "other objects of public improvement," including "public education" by name, belong to the same class of powers. In fact, not only public instruction, but hospitals, establishments of science and art, libraries, and, indeed, everything appertaining to the internal welfare of the country, are just as much objects of internal improvement, or, in other words, of internal utility, as canals and railways.

The admission of the power in either of its senses implies its existence in the other; and since if it exists at all it involves dangerous augmentation of the political functions and of the patronage of the Federal Government, we ought to see clearly by what clause or clauses of the Constitution it is conferred.

I have had occasion more than once to express, and deem it proper now to repeat, that it is, in my judgment, to be taken for granted, as a fundamental proposition not requiring elucidation, that the Federal

Government is the creature of the individual States and of the people of the States severally; that the sovereign power was in them alone; that all the powers of the Federal Government are derivative ones, the enumeration and limitations of which are contained in the instrument which organized it; and by express terms "the powers not delegated to the United States by the Constitution nor prohibited by it to the States are reserved to the States respectively or to the people."

Starting from this foundation of our constitutional faith and proceeding to inquire in what part of the Constitution the power of making appropriations for internal improvements is found, it is necessary to reject all idea of there being any grant of power in the preamble. When that instrument says, "We, the people of the United States, in order to form a more perfect union, establish justice, insure domestic tranquility, provide for the common defense, promote the general welfare, and secure the blessings of liberty to ourselves and our posterity," it only declares the inducements and the anticipated results of the things ordained and established by it. To assume that anything more can be designed by the language of the preamble would be to convert all the body of the Constitution, with its carefully weighed enumerations and limitations, into mere surplusage. The same may be said of the phrase in the grant of the power to Congress "to pay the debts and provide for the common defense and general welfare of the United States;" or, to construe the words more exactly, they are not significant of grant or concession, but of restriction of the specific grants, having the effect of saying that in laying and collecting taxes for each of the precise objects of power granted to the General Government Congress must exercise any such definite and undoubted power in strict subordination to the purpose of the common defense and general welfare of all the States.

There being no specific grant in the Constitution of a power to sanction appropriations for internal improvements, and no general provision broad enough to cover any such indefinite object, it becomes necessary to look for particular powers to which one or another of the things included in the phrase "internal improvements" may be referred. . . .

If an appropriation for improving the navigability of a river or deepening or protecting a harbor have reference to military or naval purposes, then its rightfulness, whether in amount or in the objects to which it is applied, depends, manifestly, on the military or naval exigency; and the subject-matter affords its own measure of legislative discretion. But if the appropriation for such an object have no distinct relation to the military or naval wants of the country, and is wholly, or even mainly, intended to promote the revenue from commerce, then the very vagueness of the proposed purpose of the expenditure constitutes a perpetual admonition of reserve and caution. Through disregard of this it is undeniable that in many cases appropriations of this nature have been made unwisely, without accomplishing beneficial results commensurate with the cost, and sometimes for evil rather than good, independently of their dubious relation to the Constitution.

Among the radical changes of the course of legislation in these matters which, in my judgment, the public interest demands, one is a return to the primitive idea of Congress, which required in this class of public works, as in all others, a conveyance of the soil and a cession of the jurisdiction to the United States. I think this condition ought never to have been waived in the case of any harbor improvement of a permanent nature, as where piers, jetties, sea walls, and other like works are to be constructed and maintained. It would powerfully tend to counteract endeavors to obtain appropriations of a local character and chiefly calculated to promote individual interests. The want of such a provision is the occasion of abuses in regard to existing works, exposing them to private encroachment without sufficient means of redress by law. Indeed, the absence in such cases of a cession of jurisdiction has constituted one of the constitutional objections to appropriations of this class. It is not easy to perceive any sufficient reason for requiring it in the case of arsenals or forts which does not equally apply to all other public works. If to be constructed and maintained by Congress in the exercise of a constitutional power of appropriation, they should be brought within the jurisdiction of the United States.

There is another measure of precaution in regard to such appropriations which seems to me to be worthy of the consideration of Congress. It is to make appropriation for every work in a separate bill, so that each one shall stand on its own independent merits, and if it pass shall do so under circumstances of legislative scrutiny entitling it to be regarded as of general interest and a proper subject of charge on the Treasury of the Union.

During that period of time in which the country had not come to look to Congress for appropriations of this nature several of the States whose productions or geographical position invited foreign commerce had entered upon plans for the improvement of their harbors by themselves and through means of support drawn directly from that commerce, in virtue of an express constitutional power, needing for its exercise only the permission of Congress. Harbor improvements thus constructed and maintained, the expenditures upon them being defrayed by the very facilities they afford, are a voluntary charge on those only who see fit to avail themselves of such facilities, and can be justly complained of by none. On the other hand, so long as these improvements are carried on by appropriations from the Treasury the benefits will continue to inure to those alone who enjoy the facilities afforded, while the expenditure will be a burden upon the whole country and the discrimination a double injury to places equally requiring improvement, but not equally favored by appropriations.

These considerations, added to the embarrassments of the whole question, amply suffice to suggest the policy of confining appropriations by the General Government to works necessary to the execution of its undoubted powers and of leaving all others to individual enterprise or to the separate States, to be provided for out of their own resources or by recurrence to the provision of the Constitution which authorizes the States to lay duties of tonnage with the consent of Congress.

FRANKLIN PIERCE.

ST PRIVATE CITIZENS CONDUCTING
NTRAL AMERICAN TERRITORIES

anuary 18, 1854
May 31, 1854
ecember 8, 1855

ublesome aspects in conducting
h confronted Pierce was the re-
editions against various Central
private American citizens. A-
nstances of filibusters (as such
e ones led by William Walker
caraugua and by John A. Quit-
re especially notorious. Below
tions issued by Pierce in con-
ticular filibusters. The admin-
peared to be firm measures to
ct that they took place never-
e efforts were limited. In any
southern neighbors as well as
a result of these incidents.

citizens of
organizing
island of

LAMATION.

received by me that an unlawful expe-
te of California with a view to invade
endly relations with the United States,
nizing within the United States for the

nd express
derogatory
duties and

abitants of this country, unmindful of
f the rights of a friendly power, have
ate in these enterprises, so derogatory
hreatening to our tranquility, and are
ies imposed by law against such of-

ited States
ce or war,
ny pretense

, President of the United States, have
g all persons who shall connect them-
pedition that the penalties of the law
nduct will be rigidly enforced; and I
gard our national character, as they
ions, as they value the blessings of
ntry, to discountenance and by all
terprises; and I call upon all officers

cter within
nited States
anor by an

Constitution
ion to warn
and duty to
citizens, the
quility, from
ute with due
ntry's fame,
obligations.

of this Government, civil and military, to use any efforts w
in their power to arrest for trial and punishment every such o

Given under my hand and the seal of the United States, at
(SEAL.)   this 18th day of January, A.D. 1854, and the s
of the Independence of the United States.

FRANKLIN PIE

By the President:
  W.L. MARCY,
    Secretary of State.

BY THE PRESIDENT OF THE UNITED STATE

A PROCLAMATION.

Whereas information has been received that sundry perso
the United States and others residing therein, are engaged
and fitting out a military expedition for the invasion of
Cuba; and

Whereas the said undertaking is contrary to the spiri
stipulations of treaties between the United States and Spai
to the character of this nation, and in violation of the obvio
obligations of faithful and patriotic citizens; and

Whereas it is the duty of the constituted authorities of the
to hold and maintain the control of the great question of
and not suffer the same to be lawlessly complicated under
whatever; and

Whereas to that end all private enterprises of a hostile ch
the United States against any foreign power with which the
are at peace are forbidden and declared to be a high misde
express act of Congress:

Now, therefore, in virtue of the authority vested by th
in the President of the United States, I do issue this proclam
all persons that the General Government claims it as a righ
interpose itself for the honor of its flag, the rights of i
national security, and the preservation of the public tra
whatever quarter menaced, and it will not fail to pros
energy all those who, unmindful of their own and their c
presume thus to disregard the laws of the land and our trea

I earnestly exhort all good citizens to discountenance and prevent any movement in conflict with law and national faith, especially charging the several district attorneys, collectors, and other officers of the United States, civil or military, having lawful power in the premises, to exert the same for the purpose of maintaining the authority and preserving the peace of the United States.

Given under my hand and the seal of the United States, at Washington, (SEAL.) the 31st day of May, A.D. 1854, and the seventy-eighth of the Independence of the United States.

FRANKLIN PIERCE.

By the President:
W.L. MARCY,
Secretary of State.

December 8, 1855

BY THE PRESIDENT OF THE UNITED STATES OF AMERICA.

A PROCLAMATION.

Whereas information has been received by me that sundry persons, citizens of the United States and others resident therein, are preparing, within the jurisdiction of the same, to enlist, or enter themselves, or to hire or retain others to participate in military operations within the State of Nicaragua:

Now, therefore, I, Franklin Pierce, President of the United States, do warn all persons against connecting themselves with any such enterprise or undertaking, as being contrary to their duty as good citizens and to the laws of their country and threatening to the peace of the United States.

I do further admonish all persons who may depart from the United States, either singly or in numbers, organized or unorganized, for any such purpose, that they will thereby cease to be entitled to the protection of this Government.

I exhort all good citizens to discountenance and prevent any such disreputable and criminal undertaking as aforesaid, charging all officers, civil and military, having lawful power in the premises, to exercise the same for the purpose of maintaining the authority and enforcing the laws of the United States.

In testimony whereof I have hereunto set my hand and caused the seal (SEAL.) of the United States to be affixed to these presents.

Done at the city of Washington, the 8th day of December, 1855, and of the Independence of the United States the eightieth:

FRANKLIN PIERCE.

By the President:
W.L. MARCY,
Secretary of State.

THIRD ANNUAL MESSAGE.
December 31, 1855

The late appearance of this Message was the result of a "cold war" going on between Congress and Pierce during the past year. As the address indicates at the outset, the President was presenting it even though Congress had not advised him "of their readiness to receive it."

In preparing the document, Pierce was looking ahead to his renomination in 1856 (which was not then likely and which in fact did not materialize). He was thus aiming to show his leadership and it was therefore a strongly-written message. Giving little space to the recommendations of his Cabinet, he devoted the message to two issues: the British situation in Central America, about which he was optimistic for an amicable settlement; the dominating domestic political issue, slavery, about which he was pessimistic. On the latter issue, he took the position that the Southern states had a constitutionally-protected right in the instition of slavery.

Fellow-Citzens of the Senate and of the House of Representatives:
The Constitution of the United States provides that Congress shall assemble annually on the first Monday of December, and it has been usual for the President to make no communication of a public character to the Senate and House of Representatives until advised of their readiness to receive it. I have deferred to this usage until the close of the first month of the session, but my convictions of duty will not permit me longer to postpone the discharge of the obligation enjoined by the Constitution upon the President "to give to the Congress information of the state of the Union and recommend to their consideration such measures as he shall judge ncessary and expedient."

It is matter of congratulation that the Republic is tranquilly advancing in a career of prosperity and peace.

Whilst relations of amity continue to exist between the United States and all foreign powers, with some of them grave questions are depending which may require the consideration of Congress.

Of such questions, the most important is that which has arisen out of the negotiations with Great Britain in reference to Central America.

By the convention concluded between the two Governments on the 19th of April, 1850, both parties covenanted that "neither will ever" "occupy, or fortify, or colonize, or assume or exercise any dominion over Nicaragua, Costa Rica, the Mosquito Coast, or any part of Central America."

It was the undoubted understanding of the United States in making this treaty that all the present States of the former Republic of Central America and the entire territory of each would thenceforth enjoy complete independence, and that both contracting parties engaged equally and to the same extent, for the present and for the future, that if either then had any claim of right in Central America such claim and all occupation or authority under it were unreservedly relinquished by the stipulations of the convention, and that no dominion was thereafter to be exercised or assumed in any part of Central America by Great Britain or the United States.

This Government consented to restrictions in regard to a region of country wherein we had specific and peculiar interests only upon the conviction that the like restrictions were in the same sense obligatory on Great Britain. But for this understanding of the force and effect of the convention it would never have been concluded by us.

So clear was this understanding on the part of the United States that in correspondence contemporaneous with the ratification of the convention it was distinctly expressed that the mutual covenants of nonoccupation were not intended to apply to the British establishment at the Balize. This qualification is to be ascribed to the fact that, in virtue of successive treaties with previous sovereigns of the country, Great Britain had obtained a concession of the right to cut mahogany or dye-woods at the Balize, but with positive exclusion of all domain or sovereignty; and thus it confirms the natural construction and understood import of the treaty as to all the rest of the region to which the stipulations applied.

It, however, became apparent at an early day after entering upon the discharge of my present functions that Great Britain still continued in the exercise or assertion of large authority in all that part of Central America commonly called the Mosquito Coast, and covering the entire length of the State of Nicaragua and a part of Costa Rica; that she regarded the Balize as her absolute domain and was gradually extending its limits at the expense of the State of Honduras, and that she had formally colonized a considerable insular group known as the Bay Islands, and belonging of right to that State.

All these acts or pretensions of Great Britain, being contrary to the rights of the States of Central America and to the manifest tenor of her stipulations with the United States as understood by this Government, have been made the subject of negotiation through the American minister in London. . . .

To a renewed call by this Government upon Great Britain to abide by and carry into effect the stipulations of the convention according to its obvious import by withdrawing from the possession or colonization of portions of the Central American States of Honduras, Nicaragua, and Costa Rica, the British Government has at length replied, affirming that the operation of the treaty is prospective only and did not require Great Britain to abandon or contract any possessions held by her in Central America at the date of its conclusion.

This reply substitutes a partial issue in the place of the general one presented by the United States. The British Government passes over the question of the rights of Great Britain, real or supposed, in Central America, and assumes that she had such rights at the date of the treaty and that those rights comprehended the protectorship of the Mosquito Indians, the extended jurisdiction and limits of the Balize, and the colony of the Bay Islands, and thereupon proceeds by implication to infer that if the stipulations of the treaty be merely future in effect Great Britain may still continue to hold the contested portions of Central America. The United States can not admit either the inference or the premises. We steadily deny that at the date of the treaty Great Britain had any possessions there other than the limited and peculiar establishment at the Balize, and maintain that if she had any they were surrendered by the convention.

This Government, recognizing the obligations of the treaty, has, of course, desired to see it executed in good faith by both parties, and in the discussion, therefore, has not looked to rights which we might assert independently of the treaty in consideration of our geographical position and of other circumstances which create for us relations to the Central American States different from those of any government of Europe.

The British Government, in its last communication, although well knowing the views of the United States, still declares that it sees no reason why a conciliatory spirit may not enable the two Governments to overcome all obstacles to a satisfactory adjustment of the subject.

Assured of the correctness of the construction of the treaty constantly adhered to by this Government and resolved to insist on the rights of the United States, yet actuated also by the same desire which is avowed by the British Government, to remove all causes of serious misunderstanding between two nations associated by so many ties of interest and kindred, it has appeared to me proper not to consider an amicable solution of the controversy hopeless. . . .

One other subject of discussion between the United States and Great Britain has grown out of the attempt, which the exigencies of the war in which she is engaged with Russia induced her to make, to draw recruits from the United States.

It is the traditional and settled policy of the United States to maintain impartial neutrality duringdhe wars which from time to time occur among the great powers of the world. Performing all the duties of neutrality toward the respective belligerent states, we may reasonably expect them not to interfere with our lawful enjoyment of its benefits. Notwithstanding the existence of such hostilities, our citizens retained the individual right to continue all their accustomed pursuits, by land or by sea, at home or abroad, subject only to such restrictions in this relation as the laws of war, the usage of nations, or special treaties may impose; and it is our sovereign right that our territory and jurisdiction shall not be invaded by either of the belligerent parties for the transit of their armies, the operations of their fleets, the levy of troops for their service, the fitting out of cruisers by or against either, or any other act or incident of war. And these undeniable rights of neutrality, individual and national, the United States will under no circumstances surrender. . . .

But our municipal law, in accordance with the law of nations, peremptorily forbids not only foreigners, but our own citizens, to fit out within the United States a vessel to commit hostilities against any state with which the United States are at peace, or to increase the force of any foreign armed vessel intended for such hostilities against a friendly state.

Whatever concern may have been felt by either of the belligerent powers lest private armed cruisers or other vessels in the service of one might be fitted out in the ports of this country to depredate on the property of the other, all such fears have proved to be utterly groundless. Our citizens have been withheld from any such act or purpose by good faith and by respect for the law.

While the laws of the Union are thus peremptory in their prohibition of the equipment or armament of belligerent cruisers in our ports, they provide not less absolutely that no person shall, within the territory or jurisdiction of the United States, enlist or enter himself, or hire or retain another person to enlist or enter himself, or to go beyond the limits or jurisdiction of the United States with intent to be enlisted or entered, in the service of any foreign state, either as a soldier or as a marine or seaman on board of any vessel of war, letter of marque, or privateer. And these enactments are also in strict conformity with the law of nations, which declares that no state has the right to raise troops for land or sea service in another state without its consent, and that, whether forbidden by the municipal law or not, the very attempt to do it without such consent is an attack on the national sovereignty. . . .

It is difficult to understand how it should have been supposed that troops could be raised here by Great Britain without violation of the municipal law. The unmistakable object of the law was to prevent every such act which if performed must be either in violation of the law or in studied evasion of it, and in either alternative the act done would be alike injurious to the sovereignty of the United States.

In the meantime the matter acquired additional importance by the recruitments in the United States not being discontinued, and the disclosure of the fact that they were prosecuted upon a systematic plan devised by official authority; that recruiting rendezvous had been opened in our principal cities and depots for the reception of recruits established on our frontier, and the whole business conducted under the supervision and by the regular cooperation of British officers, civil and military, some in the North American Provinces and some in the United States. The complicity of those officers in an undertaking which could only be accomplished by defying our laws, throwing suspicion over our attitude of neutrality, and disregarding our territorial rights is conclusively proved by the evidence elicited on the trial of such of their agents as have been apprehended and convicted. Some of the officers thus implicated are of high official position, and many of them beyond our jurisdiction, so that legal proceedings could not reach the source of the mischief.

These considerations, and the fact that the cause of complaint was not a mere casual occurrence, but a deliberate design, entered upon with full knowledge of our laws and national policy and conducted by responsible public functionaries, impelled me to present the case to the British Government, in order to secure not only a cessation of the wrong, but its reparation. The subject is still under discussion, the result of which will be communicated to you in due time.

I repeat the recommendation submitted to the last Congress, that provision be made for the appointment of a commissioner, in connection with Great Britain, to survey and establish the boundary line which divides the Territory of Washington from the contiguous British possessions. By reason of the extent and importance of the country in dispute, there has been imminent danger of collision between the subjects of Great Britain and the citizens of the United States, including their respective authorities, in that quarter. The prospect of a speedy arrangement has contributed hitherto to induce on both sides forbearance to assert by force what each claims as a right. Continuance of delay on the part of the two Governments to act in the matter will increase the dangers and difficulties of the controversy. . . .

With Spain peaceful relations are still maintained, and some progress has been made in securing the redress of wrongs complained of by this Government. Spain has not only disavowed and disapproved the conduct of the officers who illegally seized and detained the steamer *Black Warrior* at Havana, but has also paid the sum claimed as indemnity for the loss thereby inflicted on citizens of the United States. . . . I do not abandon the hope of concluding with Spain some general arrangement which, does not wholly present the recurrence of difficulties in Cuba, will render the less frequent, and, whenever they shall occur, facilitate their more speedy settlement. . . .

In regard to the American Republics, which from their proximity and other considerations have peculiar relations to this Government, while it has been my constant aim strictly to observe all the obligations of political friendship and of good neighborhood, obstacles to this have arisen in some of them from their own insufficient power to check lawless irruptions, which in effect throws most of the task on the United States. Thus it is that the distracted internal condition of the State of Nicaragua has made it incumbent on me to appeal to the good faith of our citizens to abstain from unlawful intervention in its affairs and to adopt preventive measures to the same end, which on a similar occasion had the best results in reassuring the peace of the Mexican States of Sonora and Lower California. . . .

Derived, as our public revenue is, in chief part from duties on imports, its magnitude affords gratifying evidence of the prosperity, not only of our commerce, but of the other great interests upon which that depends.

The principle that all moneys not required for the current expenses of the Government should remain for active employment in the hands of the people and the conspicuous fact that the annual revenue from all sources exceeds by many millions of dollars the amount needed for a prudent and economical administration of public affairs can not fail to suggest the propriety of an early revision and reduction of the tariff of duties on imports. . . .

The Army during the past year has been actively engaged in defending the Indian frontier, the state of the service permitting but few and small garrisons in our permanent fortifications. The additional regiments authorized at the last session of Congress have been recruited and organized, and a large portion of the troops have already been sent to the field. All the duties which devolve on the military establishment have been satisfactorily performed, and the dangers and privations incident to the character of the service required of our troops have furnished additional evidence of their courage, zeal, and capacity to meet any requisition which their country may make upon them. For the details of the military operations, the distribution of the troops, and additional provisions required for the military service, I refer to the report of the Secretary of War and the accompanying documents. . . .

In the Territory of Kansas there have been acts prejudicial to good order, but as yet none have occurred under circumstances to justify the interposition of the Federal Executive. That could only be in case of obstruction to Federal law or of organized resistance to Territorial law, assuming the character of insurrection, which, if it should occur, it would be my duty promptly to overcome and suppress. I cherish the hope, however, that the occurrence of any such untoward event will be prevented by the sound sense of the people of the Territory, who by its organic law, possessing the right to determine their own domestic institutions, are entitled while deporting themselves peacefully to the free exercise of that right, and must be protected in the enjoyment of it without interference on the part of the citizens of any of the States. . . .

I have thus passed in review the general state of the Union, including such particular concerns of the Federal Government, whether of domestic or foreign relation, as it appeared to me desirable and useful to bring to the special notice of Congress. Unlike the great States of Europe and

Asia and many of those of America, these United States are wasting their strength neither in foreign war nor domestic strife. Whatever of discontent or public dissatisfaction exists is attributable to the imperfections of human nature or is incident to all governments, however perfect, which human wisdom can devise. Such subjects of political agitation as occupy the public mind consist to a great extent of exaggeration of inevitable evils, or overzeal in social improvement, or mere imagination of grievance, having but remote connection with any of the constitutional functions or duties of the Federal Government. To whatever extent these questions exhibit a tendency menacing to the stability of the Constitution or the integrity of the Union, and no further, they demand the consideration of the Executive and require to be presented by him to Congress.

Before the thirteen colonies became a confederation of independent States they were associated only by community of transatlantic origin, by geographical position, and by the mutual tie of common dependence on Great Britain. When that tie was sundered they severally assumed the powers and rights of absolute self-government. The municipal and social institutions of each, its laws of property and of personal relation, even its political organization, were such only as each one chose to establish, wholly without interference from any other. In the language of the Declaration of Independence, each State had "full power to levy war, conclude peace, contract alliances, establish commerce, and to do all other acts and things which independent states may of right do." The several colonies differed in climate, in soil, in natural productions, in religion, in systems of education, in legislation, and in the forms of political administration, and they continued to differ in these respects when they voluntarily allied themselves as States to carry on the War of the Revolution.

The object of that war was to disenthrall the united colonies from foreign rule, which had proved to be oppressive, and to separate them permanently from the mother country. The political result was the foundation of a Federal Republic of the free white men of the colonies, constituted, as they were, in distinct and reciprocally independent State governments. As for the subject races, whether Indian or African, the wise and brave statesmen of that day, being engaged in no extravagant scheme of social change, left them as they were, and thus preserved themselves and their posterity from the anarchy and the ever-recurring civil wars which have prevailed in other revolutionized European colonies of America.

When the confederated States found it convenient to modify the conditions of their association by giving to the General Government direct access in some respects to the people of the States, instead of confining it to action on the States as such, they proceeded to frame the existing Constitution, adhering steadily to one guiding thought, which was to delegate only such power as was necessary and proper to the execution of specific purposes, or, in other words, to retain as much as possible consistently with those purposes of the independent powers of the individual States. For objects of common defense and security, they intrusted to the General Government certain carefully defined functions, leaving all others as the undelegated rights of the separate independent sovereignties. . . .

The Congress of the United States is in effect that congress of sovereignties which good men in the Old World have sought for, but could never attain, and which imparts to America an exemption from the mutable leagues for common action, from the wars, the mutual invasions, and vague aspirations after the balance of power which convulse from time to time the Governments of Europe. Our cooperative action rests in the conditions of permanent confederation prescribed by the Constitution. Our balance of power is in the separate reserved rights of the States and their equal representation in the Senate. That independent sovereignty in every one of the States, with its reserved rights of local self-government assured to each by their coequal power in the Senate, was the fundamental condition of the Constitution. Without it the Union would never have existed. However desirous the larger States might be to reorganize the Government so as to give to their population its proportionate weight in the common counsels, they knew it was impossible unless they conceded to the smaller ones authority to exercise at least a negative influence on all the measures of the Government, whether legislative or executive, through their equal representation in the Senate. Indeed, the larger States themselves could not have failed to perceive that the same power was equally necessary to them for the security of their own domestic interests against the aggregate force of the General Government. In a word, the original States went into this permanent league on the agreed premises of exerting their common strength for the defense of the whole and of all its parts, but of utterly excluding all capability of reciprocal aggression. Each solemnly bound itself to all the others neither to undertake nor permit any encroachment upon or intermeddling with another's reserved rights.

Where it was deemed expedient particular rights of the States were expressly guaranteed by the Constitution, but in all things besides these rights were guarded by the limitation of the powers granted and by express reservation of all powers not granted in the compact of union. Thus the great power of taxation was limited to purposes of common defense and general welfare, excluding objects appertaining to the local legislation of the several States; and those purposes of general welfare and common defense were afterwards defined by specific enumeration as being matters only of co-relation between the States themselves or between them and foreign governments, which, because of their common and general nature, could not be left to the separate control of each State.

Of the circumstances of local condition, interest, and rights in which a portion of the States, constituting one great section of the Union, differed from the rest and from another section, the most important was the peculiarity of a larger relative colored population in the Southern than in the Northern States.

A population of this class, held in subjection, existed in nearly all the States, but was more numerous and of more serious concernment in the South than in the North on account of natural differences of climate and production; and it was foreseen that, for the same reasons, while this population would diminish and sooner or later cease to exist in some States, it might increase in others. The peculiar character and magnitude of this question of local rights, not in material relations only, but still more in social ones, caused it to enter into the special stipulations of the Constitution.

Hence, while the General Government, as well by the enumerated powers granted to it as by those not enumerated, and therefore refused to it, was forbidden to touch this matter in the sense of attack or offense, it was placed under the general safeguard of the Union in the sense of defense against either invasion or domestic violence, like all other local interests of the several States. Each State expressly stipulated, as well for itself as for each and all of its citizens, and every citizen of each State became solemnly bound by his allegiance to the Constitution that any person held to service or labor in one State, escaping into another, should not, in consequence of any law or regulation thereof, be discharged from such service or labor, but should be delivered up on claim of the party to whom such service or labor might be due by the laws of his State.

Thus and thus only, by the reciprocal guaranty of all the rights of every State against interference on the part of another, was the present form of government established by our fathers and transmitted to us, and by no other means is it possible for it to exist. If one State ceases to respect the rights of another and obtrusively intermeddles with its local interests; if a portion of the States assume to impose their institutions on the others or refuse to fulfill their obligations to them, we are no longer united, friendly States, but distracted, hostile ones, with little capacity left of common advantage, but abundant means of reciprocal injury and mischief. Practically it is immaterial whether aggressive interference between the States or deliberate refusal on the part of any one of them to comply with constitutional obligations arise from erroneous conviction or blind prejudice, whether it be perpetrated by direction or indirection. In either case it is full of threat and of danger to the durability of the Union.

Placed in the office of Chief Magistrate as the executive agent of the whole country, bound to take care that the laws be faithfully executed, and specially enjoined by the Constitution to give information to Congress on the state of the Union, it would be palpable neglect of duty on my part to pass over a subject like this, which beyond all things at the present time vitally concerns individual and public security.

It has been matter of painful regret to see States conspicuous for their services in founding this Republic and equally sharing its advantages disregard their constitutional obligations to it. Although conscious of their inability to heal admitted and palpable social evils of their own, and which are completely within their jurisdiction, they engage in the offensive and hopeless undertaking of reforming the domestic institutions of other States, wholly beyond their control and authority. In the vain pursuit of ends by them entirely unattainable, and which they may not legally attempt to compass, they peril the very existence of the Constitution and all the countless benefits which it has conferred. While the people of the Southern States confine their attention to their own affairs, not presuming officiously to intermeddle with the social institutions of the Northern States, too many of the inhabitants of the latter are permanently organized in associations to inflict injury on the former by wrongful acts, which would be cause of war as between foreign powers and only fail to be such in our system because perpetrated under cover of the Union.

Is it possible to present this subject as truth and the occasion require without noticing the reiterated but groundless allegation that the South has persistently asserted claims and obtained advantages in the practical administration of the General Government to the prejudice of the North, and in which the latter has acquiesced? That is, the States which either promote or tolerate attacks on the rights of persons and of property in other States, to disguise their own injustice, pretend or imagine, and constantly aver, that they, whose constitutional rights are thus systematically assailed, are themselves the aggressors. At the present time this imputed aggression, resting, as it does, only in the vague declamatory charges of political agitators, resolves itself into misapprehension or misinterpretation, of the principles and facts of the political organization of the new Territories of the United States.

What is the voice of history? When the ordinance which provided for the government of the territory northwest of the river Ohio and for its eventual subdivision into new States was adopted in the Congress of the Confederation, it is not to be supposed that the question of future relative power as between the States which retained and those which did not retain a numerous colored population escaped notice or failed to be considered. And yet the concession of that vast territory to the interests and opinions of the Northern States, a territory now the seat of five among the largest members of the Union, was in great measure the act of the State of Virginia and of the South.

When Louisiana was acquired by the United States, it was an acquisition not less to the North than to the South; for while it was important to the country at the mouth of the river Mississippi to become the emporium of the country above it, so also it was even more important to the whole Union to have that emporium; and although the new province, by reason of its imperfect settlement, was mainly regarded as on the Gulf of Mexico, yet in fact it extended to the opposite boundaries of the United States, with far greater breadth above than below, and was in territory, as in everything else, equally at least an accession to the Northern States. It is mere delusion and prejudice, therefore, to speak of Louisiana as acquisition in the special interest of the South.

The patriotic and just men who participated in that act were influenced by motives far above all sectional jealousies. It was in truth the great event which, by completing for us the possession of the Valley of the Mississippi, with commercial access to the Gulf of Mexico, imparted unity and strength to the whole Confederation and attached together by indissoluble ties the East and the West, as well as the North and the South.

As to Florida, that was but the transfer by Spain to the United States of territory on the east side of the river Mississippi in exchange for large territory which the United States transferred to Spain on the west side of that river, as the entire diplomatic history of the transaction serves to demonstrate. Moreover, it was an acquisition demanded by the commercial interests and the security of the whole Union.

In the meantime the people of the United States had grown up to a proper consciousness of their strength, and in a brief contest with France and in a second serious war with Great Britain they had shaken off all which remained of undue reverence for Europe, and emerged from the atmosphere of those transatlantic influences which surrounded the infant Republic, and had begun to turn their attention to the full and systematic development of the internal resources of the Union.

Among the evanescent controversies of that period the most conspicuous was the question of regulation by Congress of the social condition of the future States to be founded in the territory of Louisiana.

The ordinance for the government of the territory northwest of the river Ohio had contained a provision which prohibited the use of servile labor therein, subject to the condition of the extraditions of fugitives from service due in any other part of the United States. Subsequently to the adoption of the Constitution this provision ceased to remain as a law, for its operation as such was absolutely superseded by the Constitution. But the recollection of the fact excited the zeal of social propagandism in some sections of the Confederation, and when a second State, that of Missouri, came to be formed in the territory of Louisiana proposition was made to extend to the latter territory the restriction originally applied to the country situated between the rivers Ohio and Mississippi.

Most questionable as was this proposition in all its constitutional relations, nevertheless it received the sanction of Congress, with some slight modifications of line, to save the existing rights of the intended new State. It was reluctantly acquiesced in by Southern States as a sacrifice to the cause of peace and of the Union, not only of the rights stipulated by the treaty of Louisiana, but of the principle of equality among the States guaranteed by the Constitution. It was received by the Northern States with angry and resentful condemnation and complaint, because it did not concede all which they had exactingly demanded. Having passed through the forms of legislation, it took its place in the statute book, standing open to repeal, like any other act of doubtful constitutionality, subject to be pronounced null and void by the courts of law, and possessing no possible efficacy to control the rights of the States which might thereafter be organized out of any part of the original territory of Louisiana.

In all this, if any aggression there were, any innovation upon preexisting rights, to which portion of the Union are they justly chargeable?

This controversy passed away with the occasion, nothing surviving it save the dormant letter of the statute.

But long afterwards, when by the proposed accession of the Republic of Texas the United States were to take their next step in territorial greatness, a similar contingency occurred and became the occasion for systematized attempts to intervene in the domestic affairs of one section of the Union, in defiance of their rights as States and of the stipulations of the Constitution. These attempts assumed a practical direction in the shape of persevering endeavors by some of the Representatives in both Houses of Congress to deprive the Southern States of the supposed benefit of the provisions of the act authorizing the organization of the State of Missouri.

But the good sense of the people and the vital force of the Constitution triumphed over sectional prejudice and the political errors of the day, and the State of Texas returned to the Union as she was, with social institutions which her people had chosen for themselves and with express agreement by the reannexing act that she should be susceptible of subdivision into a plurality of States.

Whatever advantage the interests of the Southern States, as such, gained by this were far inferior in results, as they unfolded in the progress of time, to those which sprang from previous concessions made by the South.

To every thoughtful friend of the Union, to the true lovers of their country, to all who longed and labored for the full success of this great experiment of republican institutions, it was cause of gratulation that such an opportunity had occurred to illustrate our advancing power on this continent and to furnish to the world additional assurance of the strength and stability of the Constitution. Who would wish to see Florida still a European colony? Who would rejoice to hail Texas as a lone star instead of one in the galaxy of States? Who does not appreciate the incalculable benefits of the acquisition of Louisiana? And yet narrow views and sectional purposes would inevitably have excluded them all from the Union.

But another struggle on the same point ensued when our victorious armies returned from Mexico and it devolved on Congress to provide for the territories acquired by the treaty of Guadalupe Hidalgo. The great relations of the subject had now become distinct and clear to the perception of the public mind, which appreciated the evils of sectional controversy upon the question of the admission of new States. In that crisis intense solicitude pervaded the nation. But the patriotic impulses of the popular heart, guided by the admonitory advice of the Father of his Country, rose superior to all the difficulties of the incorporation of a new empire into the Union. In the counsels of Congress there was manifested extreme antagonism of opinion and action between some Representatives, who sought by the abusive and unconstitutional employment of the legislative powers of the Government to interfere in the condition of the inchoate States and to impose their own social theories upon the latter, and other Representatives, who repelled the interposition of the General Government in this respect and maintained the self-constituting rights of the States. In truth, the thing attempted was in form alone action of the General Government, while in reality it was the endeavor, by abuse of legislative power, to force the ideas of internal policy entertained in particular States upon allied independent States. Once more the Constitution and the Union triumphed signally. The new territories were organized without restrictions on the disputed point, and were thus left to judge in that particular for themselves; and the sense of constitutional faith proved vigorous enough in Congress not only to accomplish this primary object, but also the incidental and hardly less important one of so amending the provisions of the statute for the extradition of fugitives from service as to place that public duty under the safeguard of the General Government, and thus relieve it from obstacles raised up by the legislation of some of the States.

Vain declamation regarding the provisions of law for the extradition of fugitives from service, with occasional episodes of frantic effort to obstruct their execution by riot and murder, continued for a brief time to agitate certain localities. But the true principle of leaving each State and Territory to regulate its own laws of labor according to its own sense of right and expediency had acquired fast hold of the public judgment, to such a degree that by common consent it was observed in the organization of the Territory of Washington.

When, more recently, it became requisite to organize the Territories of Nebraska and Kansas, it was the natural and legitimate, if not the inevitable, consequence of previous events and legislation that the same great and sound principle which had already been applied to Utah and New Mexico should be applied to them—that they should stand exempt from the restrictions proposed in the act relative to the State of Missouri.

These restrictions were, in the estimation of many thoughtful men, null from the beginning, unauthorized by the Constitution, contrary to the treaty stipulations for the cession of Louisiana, and inconsistent with the equality of these States.

They had been stripped of all moral authority by persistent efforts to procure their indirect repeal through contradictory enactments. They had been practically abrogated by the legislation attending the organization of Utah, New Mexico, and Washington. If any vitality remained in them it would have been taken away, in effect, by the new Territorial acts in the form originally proposed to the Senate at the first session of the last Congress. It was manly and ingenuous, as well as patriotic and just, to do this directly and plainly, and thus relieve the statute book of an act which might be of possible future injury, but of no possible future benefit; and the measure of its repeal was the final consummation and complete recognition of the principle that no portion of the United States shall undertake through assumption of the powers of the General Government to dictate the social institutions of any other portion.

The scope and effect of the language of repeal were not left in doubt. It was declared in terms to be "the true intent and meaning of this act not to legislate slavery into any Territory or State, nor to exclude it therefrom, but to leave the people thereof perfectly free to form and regulate their domestic institutions in their own way, subject only to the Constitution of the United States."

The measure could not be withstood upon its merits alone. It was attacked with violence on the false or delusive pretext that it constituted a breach of faith. Never was objection more utterly destitute of substantial regulative or declarative statute, whether enacted ten or forty years ago, is irrepealable; that an act of Congress is above the Constitution? If indeed, there were in the facts any cause to impute bad faith, it would attach to those only who have never ceased, from the time of the enactment of the restrictive provision to the present day, to denounce and condemn it; who have constantly refused to complete it by needful supplementary legislation; who have spared no exertion to deprive it of moral force; who have themselves again and again attempted its repeal by the enactment of incompatible provisions, and who, by the inevitable reactionary effect of their own violence on the subject, awakened the country to perception of the true constitutional principle of leaving the matter involved to the discretion of the people of the respective existing or incipient States.

It is not pretended that this principle or any other precludes the possibility of evils in practice, disturbed, as political action is liable to be, by human passions. No form of government is exempt from inconveniences; but in this case they are the result of the abuse, and not of the legitimate exercise, of the powers reserved or conferred in the organization of a Territory. They are not to be charged to the great principle of popular sovereignty. On the contrary, they disappear before the intelligence and patriotism of the people, exerting through the ballot box their peaceful and silent but irresistible power.

If the friends of the Constitution are to have another struggle, its enemies could not present a more acceptable issue than that of a State whose constitution clearly embraces "a republican form of government" being excluded from the Union because its domestic institutions may not in all respects comport with the ideas of what is wise and expedient entertained in some other State. Fresh from groundless imputations of breach of faith against others, men will commence the agitation of this new question with indubitable violation of an express compact between the independent sovereign powers of the United States and of the Republic of Texas, as well as of the older and equally solemn compacts which assure the equality of all the States.

But deplorable as would be such a violation of compact in itself and in all its direct consequences, that is the very least of the evils involved. When sectional agitators shall have succeeded in forcing on this issue, can their pretensions fail to be met by counter pretensions? Will not different States be compelled, respectively, to meet extremes with extremes? And if either extreme carry its point, what is that so far forth but dissolution of the Union? If a new State, formed from the territory of the United States, be absolutely excluded from admission therein, that fact of itself constitutes the disruption of union between it and the other States. But the process of dissolution could not stop there. Would not a sectional decision producing such result by a majority of votes, either Northern or Southern, of necessity drive out the oppressed and aggrieved minority and place in presence of each other two irreconcilably hostile confederations?

It is necessary to speak thus plainly of projects the offspring of that sectional agitation now prevailing in some of the States, which are as impracticable as they are unconstitutional, and which if persevered in must and will end calamitously. It is either disunion and civil war or it is mere angry, idle, aimless disturbance of public peace and tranquility. Disunion for what? If the passionate rage of fanaticism and partisan spirit did not force the fact upon our attention, it would be difficult to believe that any considerable portion of the people of this enlightened country could have so surrendered themselves to a fanatical devotion to the supposed interests of the relatively few Africans in the United States as totally to abandon and disregard the interests of the 25,000,000 Americans, to trample under foot the injunctions of moral and constitutional obligation, and to engage in plans of vindictive hostility against those who are associated with them in the enjoyment of the common heritage of our national institutions.

Nor is it hostility against their fellow-citizens of one section of the Union alone. The interests, the honor, the duty, the peace, and the prosperity of the people of all sections are equally involved and imperiled in this question. And are patriotic men in any part of the Union prepared on such issue thus madly to invite all the consequences of the forfeiture of their constitutional engagements? It is impossible. The storm of frenzy and faction must inevitably dash itself in vain against the unshaken rock of the Constitution. I shall never doubt it. I know that the Union is stronger a thousand times than all the wild and chimerical schemes of social change which are generated one after another in the unstable minds of visionary sophists and interested agitators. I rely confidently on the patriotism of the people, on the dignity and self-respect of the States, on the wisdom of Congress, and, above all, on the continued gracious favor of Almighty God to maintain against all enemies, whether at home or abroad, the sanctity of the Constitution and the integrity of the Union.

FRANKLIN PIERCE

SPECIAL MESSAGE ON THE PROBLEMS OF CENTRAL AMERICA AND THE AMERICAN ISTHMUS
May 15, 1856

This message was a gesture of defiance of Great Britain's presence in the Central American area. It was also a strong statement of American foreign policy in the Western Hemisphere which a contemporary student will find still plagues relations between the two Americas.

The President had spoken in his inaugural about territorial expansion and trade extension. Friction with Great Britain in Central America was an important element in Pierce's foreign policy throughout his administration, in spite of the Clayton-Bulwer Treaty in which both sides agreed to extend their interests no further in Central America and to refrain from exercising exclusive control over any canal which might be built in that region. Not only British "aggression" had to be contended with, but also the interests of American expansionists including those who represented commercial interests, Southerners who sought areas for extension of slavery, and those who simply viewed the area as necessary to United States defense and security.

WASHINGTON, *May 15, 1856.*

To the Senate and House of Representatives:

I transmit herewith reports of the Secretary of State, the Secretary of the Navy, and the Attorney-General, in reply to a resolution of the Senate of the 24th of March last, and also to a resolution of the House of Representatives of the 8th of May instant, both having reference to the routes of transit between the Atlantic and Pacific oceans through the Republics of New Granada and Nicaragua and to the condition of affairs in Central America.

These documents relate to questions of the highest importance and interest to the people of the United States.

The narrow isthmus which connects the continents of North and South America, by the facilities it affords for easy transit between the Atlantic and Pacific oceans, rendered the countries of Central America an object of special consideration to all maritime nations, which has been greatly augmented in modern times by the operation of changes in commercial relations, especially those produced by the general use of steam as a motive power by land and sea. To us, on account of its geographical position and of our political interest as an American State of primary magnitude, that isthmus is of peculiar importance, just as the Isthmus of Suez is, for corresponding reasons, to the maritime powers of Europe. But above all, the importance to the United States of securing free transit across the American isthmus has rendered it of paramount interest to us since the settlement of the Territories of Oregon and Washington and the accession of California to the Union.

Impelled by these considerations, the United States took steps at an early day to assure suitable means of commercial transit by canal railway, or otherwise across this isthmus.

We concluded, in the first place, a treaty of peace, amity, navigation, and commerce with the Republic of New Granada, among the conditions of which was a stipulation on the part of New Granada guaranteeing to the United States the right of way or transit across that part of the Isthmus which lies in the territory of New Granada, in consideration of which the United States guaranteed in respect of the same territory the rights of sovereignty and property of New Granada.

The effect of this treaty was to afford to the people of the United States facilities for at once opening a common road from Chagres to Panama and for at length constructing a railway in the same direction, to connect regularly with steamships, for the transportation of mails, specie, and passengers to and fro between the Atlantic and Pacific States and Territories of the United States.

The United States also endeavored, but unsuccessfully, to obtain from the Mexican Republic the cession of the right of way at the northern extremity of the Isthmus by Tehuantepec, and that line of communication continues to be an object of solicitude to the people of this Republic.

In the meantime, intervening between the Republic lie the States of Guatemala, Salvador, Honduras, Nicaragua, and Costa Rica, the several members of the former Republic of Central America. Here, in the territory of the Central American States, is the narrowest part of the Isthmus, and hither, of course, public attention has been directed as the most inviting field for enterprises of interoceanic communication between the opposite shores of America, and more especially to the territory of the States of Nicaragua and Honduras.

Paramount to that of any European State, as was the interest of the United States in the security and freedom of projected lines of travel across the Isthmus by the way of Nicaragua and Honduras, still we did not yield in this respect to any suggestions of territorial aggrandizement, or even of exclusive advantage, either of communication or of commerce. Opportunities had not been wanting to the United States to procure such advantage by peaceful means and with full and free assent of those who alone had any legitimate authority in the matter. We disregarded those opportunities from considerations alike of domestic and foreign policy, just as, even to the present day, we have persevered in a system of justice and respect for the rights and interests of others as well as our own in regard to each and all of the States of Central America.

It was with surprise and regret, therefore, that the United States learned a few days after the conclusion of the treaty of Guadalupe Hidalgo, by which the United States became, with the consent of the Mexican Republic, the rightful owners of California, and thus invested with augmented special interest in the political condition of Central America, that a military expedition, under the authority of the British Government, had landed at San Juan del Norte, in the State of Nicaragua, and taken forcible possession of that port, the necessary terminus of any canal or railway across the Isthmus within the territories of Nicaragua.

It did not diminish the unwelcomeness to us of this act on the part of Great Britain to find that she assumed to justify it on the ground of an alleged protectorship of a small and obscure band of uncivilized Indians, whose proper name had even become lost to history, who did not constitute a state capable of territorial sovereignty either in fact or of right, and all political interest in whom and in the territory they occupied Great Britain had previously renounced by successive treaties with Spain when Spain was sovereign to the country and subsequently with independent Spanish America.

Nevertheless, and injuriously affected as the United States conceived themselves to have been by this act of the British Government and by its occupation about the same time of insular and of continental portions of the territory of the State of Honduras, we remembered the many and powerful ties and mutual interests by which Great Britain and the United States are associated, and we proceeded in earnest good faith and with a sincere desire to do whatever might strengthen the bonds of peace between us to negotiate with Great Britain a convention to assure the perfect neutrality of all interoceanic communications across the Isthmus and, as the indispensable condition of such neutrality, the absolute independence of the States of Central America and their complete sovereignty within the limits of their own territory as well against Great Britain as against the United States. We supposed we had accomplished that object by the conventions of April 19, 1850, which would never have been signed nor ratified on the part of the United States but for the conviction that in virtue of its provisions neither Great Britain nor the United States was thereafter to exercise any territorial sovereignty in fact or in name in any part of Central America, however or whensoever acquired, either before or afterwards. The essential object of the convention—the neutralization of the Isthmus—would, of course, become a nullity if either Great Britain or the United States were to continue to hold exclusively islands or mainland of the Isthmus, and more especially if, under any claim of protectorship of Indians, either Government were to remain forever sovereign in fact of the Atlantic shores of the three States of Costa Rica, Nicaragua, and Honduras.

I have already communicated to the two Houses of Congress full information of the protracted and hitherto fruitless efforts which the United

States have made to arrange this international question with Great Britain. It is referred to on the present occasion only because of its intimate connection with the special object now to be brought to the attention of Congress.

The unsettled political condition of some of the Spanish American Republics has never ceased to be regarded by this Government with solicitude and regret on their own account, while it has been the source of continual embarrassment in our public and private relations with them. In the midst of the violent revolutions and the wars by which they are continually agitated, their public authorities are unable to afford due protection to foreigners and to foreign interests within their territory, or even to defend their own soil against individual aggressors, foreign or domestic, the burden of the inconveniences and losses of which therefore devolves in no inconsiderable degree upon the foreign states associated with them in close relations of geographical vicinity of of commercial intercourse.

Such is more emphatically the situation of the United States with respect to the Republics of Mexico and of Central America. Notwithstanding, however, the relative remoteness of the European States from America, facts of the same order have not failed to appear conspicuously in their intercourse with Spanish American Republics. Great Britain has repeatedly been constrained to recur to measures of force for the protection of British interests in those countries. France found it necessary to attack the castle of San Juan de Uloa and even to debark troops at Vera Cruz in order to obtain redress of wrongs done to Frenchmen in Mexico.

What is memorable in this respect in the conduct and policy of the United States is that while it would be as easy for us to annex and absorb new territories in America as it is for European States to do this in Asia or Africa, and while if done by us it might be justified as well on the alleged ground of the advantage which would accrue therefrom to the territories annexed and absorbed, yet we have abstained from doing it, on obedience to considerations of right not less than of policy; and that while the courageous and self-restraint spirit of our people prompts them to hardy enterprises, and they occasionally yield to the temptation of taking part in the troubles of countries near at hand, where they know how potential their influence, moral and material, must be, the American Government has uniformly and steadily resisted all attempts of individuals in the United States to undertake armed aggression against friendly Spanish American Republics.

While the present incumbent of the executive office has been in discharge of its duties he has never failed to exert all the authority in him vested to repress such enterprises, because they are in violation of the law of the land, which the Constitution requires him to execute faithfully; because they are contrary to the policy of the Government, and because to permit them would be a departure from good faith toward those American Republics in amity with us, which are entitled to, and will never cease to enjoy, in their calamities the cordial sympathy, and in their prosperity the efficient good will, of the Government and of the people of the United States.

To say that our laws in this respect are sometimes violated or success-fully evaded is only to say what is true of all laws in all countries, but not more so in the United States than in any one whatever of the coun-tries of Europe. Suffice it to repeat that the laws of the United States prohibiting all foreign military enlistments or expeditions within our ter-ritory have been executed with impartial good faith, and, so far as the nature of things permits, as well in repression of private persons as of the official agents of other Governments, both of Europe and America.

Among the Central American Republics to which modern events have imparted most prominence is that of Nicaragua, by reason of its par-ticular position on the Isthmus. Citizens of the United States have estab-lished in its territory a regular interoceanic transit route, second only in utility and value to the one previously established in the territory of New Granda. The condition of Nicaragua would, it is believed, have been much more prosperous than it has been but for the occupation of its only Atlantic port by a foreign power, and of the disturbing authority set up and sustained by the same power in a portion of its territory, by means of which its domestic sovereignty was impaired, its public lands were withheld from settlement, and it was deprived of all the maritime revenue which it would otherwise collect on imported merchandise at San Juan del Norte.

In these circumstances of the political debility of the Republic of Nica-ragua, and when its inhabitants were exhuasted by long-continued civil war between parties neither of them strong enough to overcome the other or permanently maintain internal tranquility, one of the contending fac-tions of the Republic invited the assistance and cooperation of a small body of citizens of the United States from the State of California, whose presence, as it appears, put an end at once to civil war and restored apparent order throughout the territory of Nicaragua, with a new admin-istration, having at its head a distinguished individual, by birth a citizen of the Republic, D. Patricio Rivas, as its provisional President.

It is the established policy of the United States to recognize all gov-ernments without question of their source or their organization, or of the means by which the governing persons attain their power, provided there be a government *de facto* accepted by the people of the country, and with reserve only of the time as to the recognition of revolutionary govern-ments arising out of the subdivision of parent states with which we are in relations of amity. We do not go behind the fact of a foreign govern-ment exercising actual power to investigate questions of legitimacy; we do not inquire into the causes which may have led to a change of govern-ment. To us it is indifferent whether a successful revolution has been aided by foreign intervention or not; whether insurrection has overthrown existing government, and another has been established in its place according to preexisting forms or in a manner adopted for the occasion by those whom we may find in the actual possession of power. All these matters we leave to the people and public authorities of the particular country to determine; and their determination, whether it be by positive action or by ascertained acquiescence is to us a sufficient warranty of the legitimacy of the new government.

During the sixty-seven years which have elapsed since the establishment of the existing Government of the United States, in all which time this Union has maintained undisturbed domestic tranquility, we have had occasion to recognize governments *de facto,* founded either by domestic revolution or by military invasion from abroad, in many of the Governments of Europe.

It is the more imperatively necessary to apply this rule to the Spanish American Republics, in consideration of the frequent and not seldom anomalous changes of organization or administration which they undergo and the revolutionary nature of most of these changes, of which the recent series of revolutions in the Mexican Republic is an example, where five successive revolutionary governments have made their appearance in the course of a few months and been recognized successively, each as the political power of that country, by the United States.

When, therefore, some time since, a new minister from the Republic of Nicaragua presented himself, bearing the commission of President Rivas, he must and would have been received as such, unless he was found on inquiry subject to personal exception, but for the absence of satisfactory information upon the question whether President Rivas was **in fact** the head of an established Government of the Republic of Nicaragua, doubt as to which arose not only from the circumstances of his avowed association with armed emigrants recently from the United States, but that the proposed minister himself was of that class of persons, and not otherwise or previously a citizen of Nicaragua.

Another minister from the Republic of Nicaragua has now presented himself, and has been received as such, satisfactory evidence appearing that he represents the Government *de facto* and, so far as such exists, the Government *de jure* of that Republic.

That reception, while in accordance with the established policy of the United States, was likewise called for by the most imperative special exigencies, which require that this Government shall enter at once into diplomatic relations with that of Nicaragua. In the first place, a difference has occurred between the Government of President Rivas and the Nicaragua Transit Company, which involves the necessity of inquiry into rights of citizens of the United States, who allege that they have been aggrieved by the acts of the former and claim protection and redress at the hands of their Government. In the second place, the interoceanic communication by the way of Nicaragua is effectually interrupted, and the persons and property of unoffending private citizens of the United States in that country require the attention of their Government. Neither of these objects can receive due consideration without resumption of diplomatic inter-course with the Government of Nicaragua.

Further than this, the documents communicated show that while the interoceanic transit by the way of Nicaragua is cut off, disturbances at Panama have occurred to obstruct, temporarily at least, that by the way of New Granada, involving the sacrifice of the lives and property of citizens of the United States. A special commissioner has been dispatched to Panama to investigate the facts of this occurrence with a view par-ticularly to the redress of parties aggrieved. But measures of another class will be demanded for the future security of interoceanic communi-cation by this as by the other routes of the Isthmus.

It would be difficult to suggest a single object of interest, external or internal, more important to the United States than the maintenance of the communication, by land and sea, between the Atlantic and Pacific States and Territories of the Union. It is a material element of the na-tional integrity and sovereignty.

I have adopted such precautionary measures and have taken such action for the purpose of affording security to the several transit routes of Cen-tral America and to the persons and property of citizens of the United States connected with or using the same as are within my constitutional power and as existing circumstances have seemed to demand. Should these measures prove inadequate to the object, that fact will be communicated to Congress with such recommendations as the exigency of the case may indicate.

FRANKLIN PIERCE.

FOURTH ANNUAL MESSAGE
December 2, 1856

The opening passages of this last Message reflects Pierce's feeling that the Democratic victory in the recent election was an endorsement by the people of his party, his vows, his administration. Thus the Message does not review the achievements of his administration or suggest new plans, but rather sermonizes the Republicans about the errors of their views on the matter of imposing their anti-slavery position upon the South. He indicts those who he contends are thereby leading the nation to disunion and civil war. The remainder of his message is devoted to foreign affairs, reporting that all difficulties with Great Britain were settled. He also reviewed his own efforts to influence the peace conference which closed the Crimean War. Finally, a series of platitudes on the American vision closes the document.

WASHINGTON,December 2, 1856.

Fellow-Citizens of the Senate and of the House of Representatives:

The Constitution requires that the President shall from time to time not only recommend to the consideration of Congress such measures as he may judge necessary and expedient, but also that he shall give information to them of the state of the Union. To do this fully involves exposition of all matters in the actual condition of the country, domestic or foreign, which essentially concern the general welfare. While performing his constitutional duty in this respect, the President does not speak merely to express personal convictions, but as the executive minister of the Government, enabled by his position and called upon by his official obligations to scan with an impartial eye the interests of the whole and of every part of the United States.

Of the condition of the domestic interests of the Union—its agriculture, mines, manufactures, navigation, and commerce—it is necessary only to say that the internal prosperity of the country, its continuous and steady advancement in wealth and population and in private as well as public well-being, attest the wisdom of our institutions and the predominant spirit of intelligence and patriotism which, notwithstanding occasional irregularities of opinion or action resulting from popular freedom, has distinguished and characterized the people of America.

In the brief interval between the termination of the last and the commencement of the present session of Congress the public mind has been occupied with the care of selecting for another constitutional term the

President and Vice-President of the United States.

The determination of the persons who are of right, or contingently, to preside over the administration of the Government is under our system committed to the States and the people. We appeal to them, by their voice pronounced in the forms of law, to call whomsoever they will to the high post of Chief Magistrate.

And thus it is that as the Senators represent the respective States of the Union and the members of the House of Representatives the several constituencies of each State, so the President represents the aggregate population of the United States. Their election of him is the explicit and solemn act of the sole sovereign authority of the Union.

It is impossible to misapprehend the great principles which by their recent political action the people of the United States have sanctioned and announced.

They have asserted the constitutional equality of each and all of the States of the Union as States: they have affirmed the constitutional equality of each and all of the citizens of the United States as citizens, whatever their religion, wherever their birth of their residence; they have maintained the inviolability of the constitutional rights of the different sections of the Union, and they have proclaimed their devoted and unalterable attachment to the Union and to the Constitution, as objects of interest superior to all subjects of local or sectional controversy, as the safeguard of the rights of all, as the spirit and the essence of the liberty, peace, and greatness of the Republic.

In doing this they have at the same time emphatically condemned the idea of organizing in these United States mere geographical parties, of marshaling in hostile array toward each other the different parts of the country, North or South, East or West.

Schemes of this nature, fraught with incalculable mischief, and which the considerate sense of the people has rejected, could have had countenance in no part of the country had they not been disguised by suggestions plausible in appearance, acting upon an excited state of the public mind, induced by causes temporary in their character and, it is to be hoped, transient in their influence. . . .

When my last annual message was transmitted to Congress two subjects of controversy, one relating to the enlistment of soliders in this country for foreign service and the other to Central America, threatened to disturb the good understanding between the United States and Great Britain. Of the progress and termination of the former question you were informed at the time, and the other is now in the way of satisfactory adjustment.

The object of the convention between the United States and Great Britain of the 19th of April, 1850, was to secure for the benefit of all nations the neutrality and the common use of any transit way or interoceanic communication across the Isthmus of Panama which might be opened within the limits of Central America. The pretensions subsequently asserted by Great Britain to dominion or control over territories in or near two of the routes, those of Nicaragua and Honduras, were deemed by the United States not merely incompatible with the main object of the treaty, but opposed even to its express stipulations. Occasion of controversy on this point has been removed by an additional treaty, which our minister at London has concluded, and which will be immediately submitted to the Senate for its consideration. Should the proposed supplemental arrangement be concurred in by all the parties to be affected by it, the objects contemplated by the original convention will have been fully attained.

The treaty between the United States and Great Britain of the 5th of June, 1854, which went into effective operation in 1855, put an end to causes of irritation between the two countries, by securing to the United States the right of fishery on the coast of the British North American Provinces, with advantages equal to those enjoyed by British subjects. Besides the signal benefits of this treaty to a large class of our citizens engaged in a pursuit connected to no inconsiderable degree with our national prosperity and strength, it has had a favorable effect upon other interests in the provision it made for reciprocal freedom of trade between the United States and the British Provinces in America.

The exports of domestic articles to those Provinces during the last year amounted to more than $22,000,000, exceeding those of the preceding year by nearly $7,000,000; and the imports therefrom during the same period amounted to more than twenty-one million, an increase of six million upon those of the previous year.

The improved condition of this branch of our commerce is mainly attributable to the above-mentioned treaty.

Provision was made in the first article of that treaty for a commission to designate the mouths of rivers to which the common right of fishery on the coast of the United States and the British Provinces was not to extend. This commission has been employed a part of two seasons, but without much progress in accomplishing the object for which it was instituted, in consequence of a serious difference of opinion between the commissioners, not only as to the precise point where the rivers terminate, but in many instances as to what constitutes a river. These difficulties, however, may be overcome by resort to the umpirage provided for by the treaty. . . .

With Spain no new difficulties have arisen, nor has much progress been made in the adjustment of pending ones.

Negotiations entered into for the purpose of relieving our commercial intercourse with the island of Cuba of some of its burdens and providing for the more speedy settlement of local disputes growing out of that intercourse have not yet been attended with any results . . . .

I have expressed a readiness on the part of this Government to accede to all the principles contained in the declaration of the conference of Paris provided that the one relating to the abandonment of privateering can be so amended as to effect the object for which, as is presumed, it was intended—the immunity of private property on the ocean from hostile capture. To effect this object, it is proposed to add to the declaration that "privateering is and remains abolished" the following amendment: "And that the private property of subjects and citizens of a belligerent on the high seas shall be exempt from seizure by the public armed vessels of the other belligerent, except it be contraband."

This amendment has been presented not only to the powers which have asked our assent to the declaration to abolish privateering, but to all other maritime states. Thus far it has not been rejected by any, and is favorably entertained by all which have made any communication in reply.

Several of the governments regarding with favor the proposition of the United States have delayed definitive action upon it only for the purpose of consulting with others, parties to the conference of Paris. I have the satisfaction of stating, however, that the Emperor of Russia has entirely and explicitly approved of that modification and will coöperate in endeavoring to obtain the assent of other powers, and that assurances of a similar purport have been received in relation to the disposition of the Emperor of the French.

The present aspect of this important subject allows us to cherish the hope that a principle so humane in its character, so just and equal in its operation, so essential to the prosperity of commercial nations, and so consonant to the sentiments of this enlightened period of the world will command the approbation of all maritime powers, and thus be incorporated into the code of international law . . . .

The Government of the United States has at all times regarded with friendly interest the other States of America, formerly, like this country, European colonies, and now independent members of the great family of nations. But the unsettled condition of some of them, distracted by frequent revolutions, and thus incapable of regular and firm internal administration, has tended to embarrass occasionally our public intercourse by reason of wrongs which our citizens suffer at their hands, and which they are slow to redress.

Unfortunately, it is against the Republic of Mexico, with which it is our special desire to maintain a good understanding, that such complaints are most numerous; and although earnestly urged upon its attention, they have not as yet received the consideration which this Government had a right to expect. While reparation for past injuries has been withheld, others have been added. The political condition of that country, however, has been such as to demand forbearance on the part of the United States. I shall continue my efforts to procure for the wrongs of our citizens that redress which is indispensable to the continued friendly association of the two Republics.

The peculiar condition of affairs in Nicaragua in the early part of the present year rendered it important that this Government should have diplomatic relations with that State. Through its territory had been opened one of the principal thoroughfares across the isthmus connecting North and South America, on which a vast amount of property was transported and to which our citizens resorted in great numbers in passing between the Atlantic and Pacific coasts of the United States. The protection of both required that the existing power in that State should be regarded as a responsible Government, and its minister was accordingly received. But he remained here only a short time. Soon thereafter the political affairs of Nicaragua underwent unfavorable change and became involved in much uncertainty and confusion. Diplomatic representatives from two contending parties have been recently sent to this Government, but with the imperfect information possessed it was not possible to decide which was the Government de facto, and, awaiting further developments, I have refused to receive either. . . .

The present condition of the Isthmus of Panama, in so far as regards the security of persons and property passing over it, requires serious consideration. Recent incidents tend to show that the local authorities can not be relied on to maintain the public peace of Panama, and there is just ground for apprehension that a portion of the inhabitants are meditating further outrages, without adequate measures for the security and protection of persons or property having been taken, either by the State of Panama or by the General Government of New Granada.

Under the guaranties of treaty, citizens of the United States have, by the outlay of several million dollars, constructed a railroad across the Isthmus, and it has become the main route between our Atlantic and Pacific possessions, over which multitudes of our citizens and a vast amount of property are constantly passing; to the security and protection of all which and the continuance of the public advantages involved it is impossible for the Government of the United States to be indifferent.

I have deemed the danger of the recurrence of scenes of lawless violence in this quarter so imminent as to make it my duty to station a part of our naval force in the harbors of Panama and Aspinwall, in order to protect the persons and property of the citizens of the United States in those ports and to insure to them safe passage across the Isthmus. And it would, in my judgment, be unwise to withdraw the naval force now in those ports until, by the spontaneous action of the Republic of New Granada or otherwise, some adequate arrangement shall have been made for the protection and security of a line of interoceanic communcation, so important at this time not to the United States only, but to all other maritime states, both of Europe and America.

Meanwhile negotiations have been instituted, by means of a special commission, to obtain from New Granada full indemnity for injuries sustained by our citizens on the Isthmus and satisfactory security for the general interests of the United States.

In addressing to you my last annual message the occasion seems to me an appropriate one to express my congratulations, in view of the peace, greatness, and felicity which the United States now possess and enjoy. To point you to the state of the various Departments of the Government and of all the great branches of the public service, civil and military, in order to speak of the intelligence and the integrity which pervades the whole, would be to indicate but imperfectly the administrative condition of the country and the beneficial effects of that on the general welfare. Nor would it suffice to say that the nation is actually at peace at home and abroad; that its industrial interests are prosperous; that the canvas of its mariners whitens every sea, and the plow of its husbandmen is marching steadily onward to the bloodless conquest of the continent; that cities and populous States are springing up, as if by enchantment, from the bosom of our Western wilds, and that the courageous energy of our people is making of these United States the great Republic of the world. These results have not been attained without passing through trials and perils, by experience of which, and thus only, nations can harden into manhood. Our forefathers were trained to the wisdom which conceived and the courage which achieved independence by the circumstances which surrounded them, and they were thus made capable of the creation of the Republic. It devolved on the next generation to consolidate the work of the Revolution, to deliver the country entirely from the influence of conflicting transatlantic partialities or antipathies which attached to our colonial and Revolutionary history, and to organize the practical operation of the constitutional and legal institutions of the Union. To us of this generation remains the not less noble task of maintaining and extending the national power. We have at length reached that stage of our country's career in which the dangers to be encountered and the exertions to be made are the incidents, not of weakness, but of strength. In foreign relations we have to attemper our power to the less happy condition of other Republics in America and to place ourselves in the calmness and conscious dignity of right by the side of the greatest and wealthiest of the Empires of Europe. In domestic relations we have to guard against the shock of the discontents, the ambitions, the interests, and the exuberant, and therefore sometimes irregular, impulses of opinion or of action which are the natural product of the present political elevation, the self-reliance, and the restless spirit of enterprise of the people of the United States.

I shall prepare to surrender the Executive trust to my successor and retire to private life with sentiments of profound gratitude to the good Providence which during the period of my Administration has vouch-safed to carry the country through many difficulties, domestic and foreign, and which enables me to contemplate the spectacle of amicable and respectful relations between ours and all other governments and the establishment of constitutional order and tranquility throughout the Union.

Franklin Pierce.

BIBLIOGRAPHICAL AIDS

The emphasis in this and subsequent volumes in the **Presidential Chronologies** series will be on the administrations of the presidents. The more important works on other aspects of their lives, either before or after their terms in office, are included since they may contribute to an understanding of the presidential careers.

The following biography is critically selected. Additional titles may be found in the Nichols' biography of Pierce. (See biographies below) and in the standard guide. The student might also wish to consult **Reader's Guide to Periodical Literature** and **Social Sciences and Humanities Index** (formerly **International Index)** for recent articles in scholarly journals.

Additional chronological information not included in this volume because it did not relate to the president may be found in the **Encyclopedia of American History,** edited by Richard B. Morris, revised edition (New York, 1965).

Asteriks after titles refer to books currently available in paperback editions.

SOURCE MATERIALS

Source material dealing with the Pierce administration is very limited compared to what is available on American presidents generally. The Library of Congress has 26 volumes which are available on microfilm at most university and college libraries. But this represents but a small part of what existed when Pierce left the White House. According to his biographer, Professor Nichols, he destroyed his papers for those years.

While scattered in a number of libraries throughout the country, the bulk of the Pierce manuscripts are in the Henry E. Huntington Library, San Marino, California, and in the New Hampshire Historical Society, Concord, New Hampshire.

The most accessible bibliographical aid on these sources is the **Index to the Franklin Pierce Papers,** in the Presidents' **Paper Index Series** published by the Library of Congress (1962). Another helpful bibliography of sources is Wilmer R. Leech, **Calendar of Papers of Franklin Pierce** (Washington, 1917).

For general policies of the Administration, Presidential messages and reports of the Cabinet, one should turn to Congressional documents and the archives of the departments.

It should be noted that Nathaniel Hawthorne, the New England novelist, was one of Pierce's most intimate friends since their undergraduate years at Bowdoin College. Hawthorne's autobiographical writings as well as his campaign biography of Pierce contain a good deal of source material.

BIOGRAPHY

Bartlett, David Vandewater Golden. **The Life of General Frank. Pierce, of New Hampshire, the Democratic Candidate for President of the United States.** 1852. A campaign biography.

Hawthorne, Nathaniel. **Life of Franklin Pierce.** Boston, 1852. While another campaign biography, it contains a great deal of insights on Pierce's character and personality as described by a literary master and an intimate friend of Pierce.

Nichols, Roy Franklin. **Franklin Pierce. Young Hickory of the Granite Hills.** Philadelphia, 1958. This detailed and dispassionate biography of Pierce is the only full-length biography available. It contains exhaustive notes and a complete bibliography. A splendid piece of scholarship. Revises the 1931 edition.

ESSAYS, MONOGRAPHS, and RELATED BIOGRAPHIES

Capers, G. M. **Stephen A. Douglas, Defender of the Union.** Gainesville, Florida, 1959.

Johannsen, Robert W. **The Union in Crisis, 1850-1877.** Chicago, 1965.* A fine source book of documents dealing with the period of our interest.

Klement, Frank L. "Franklin Pierce and the Treason Charges of 1861-1862," **The Historian,** XXIII (August, 1961), 436-448.

Manning, S. W. "Tragedy of the Ten-Million-Acre Bill," **Social Service Review,** XXXVI (March 6, 1962), 44-50.

Nevins, Allan. **Ordeal of the Union.** 2 volumes, New York, 1947. A definitive work which no student can overlook. Volume II deals with the Pierce administration.

Nichols, Roy F. **The Stakes of Power,** 1845-1877. New York, 1961.* Surveys and interprets major political, social, military and economic events and the significance of those events in this "middle period" of American history.

Purcell, Richard J. "Franklin Pierce: A Forgotten President," **Catholic Educational Review,** XXXI (August, 1933), 134-141.

Russel, R. R. "Issues in the Congressional Struggle Over the Kansas-Nebraska Bill, 1854," **Journal of Southern History,** XXIX (May, 1963), 187-210.

Smith, Elbert B. **The Death of Slavery: The United States, 1837-1865.** Chicago, 1967. An important revisionist study of one of the crucial issues of Pierce's time.

Strode, Hudson. **Jefferson Davis: American Patriot.** New York, 1955.

Wallace, Edward S. **Destiny and Glory.** New York, 1957. A popular written account of the deeds and adventures of various groups of Americans who made hostile expedition to the Caribbean islands, Central and South America, during the years between the Mexican and Civil Wars.

THE PRESIDENCY

Bailey, Thomas A. **Presidential Greatness: The Image and the Man from George Washington to the Present.** New York, 1966.* A critical and subjective study of the qualities of presidential greatness, arranged topically rather than chronologically. Bailey lists forty-three yardsticks for measuring presidential ability. The book includes an excellent up to date bibliography on presidential powers and problems, with special emphasis on measuring effectiveness or greatness according to the Bailey criteria.

Binkley, Wilfred E. **The Man in the White House: His Powers and Duties.** Revised ed. New York, 1964.* Treats the development of the various roles of the American president.

Brown, Stuart Gerry. **The American Presidency: Leadership, Partisanship, and Popularity.** New York, 1966.* Seems to like the more partisan presidents like Jefferson and Jackson.

Burns, James McGregor. **Presidential Government: The Crucible of Leadership.** Boston, 1966.*

Corwin, Edward S. **The President: Office and Powers.** 4th ed. New York, 1957.* An older classic.

Kane, Joseph Nathan. **Facts About the Presidents.** New York, 1959. Includes comparative as well as biographical data about the presidents.

Koenig, Louis W. **The Chief Executive.** New York, 1964. Authoritative study of presidential powers.

Laski, Harold J. **The American Presidency.** New York, 1940.* A classic.

Rossiter, Clinton. **The American Presidency.** 2nd ed. New York, 1960.* Useful.

Schlesinger, Arthur Meier. "Historians Rate United States Presidents," **Life,** XXV (November 1, 1948), 65 ff.

————. "Our Presidents: A Rating by Seventy-five Historians," **New York Times Magazine,** July 29, 1962, 12 ff.

NAME INDEX

TITLES IN THE OCEANA
PRESIDENTIAL CHRONOLOGY SERIES

Senior Editor: Howard F. Bremer

Reference books containing Chronology - Documents - Bibliographical Aids for each President covered.

1. GEORGE WASHINGTON   96 pages/$3.00
    edited by Howard F. Bremer

2. JOHN ADAMS   96 pages/$3.00
    edited by Howard F. Bremer

3. JAMES BUCHANAN   96 pages/$3.00
    edited by Irving J. Sloan

4. GROVER CLEVELAND   128 pages/$4.00
    edited by Robert I. Vexler

5. FRANKLIN PIERCE   96 pages/$3.00
    edited by Irving J. Sloan

6. ULYSSES S. GRANT   128 pages/$4.00
    edited by Philip Moran

Books may be ordered from
OCEANA PUBLICATIONS, INC.
Dobbs Ferry, New York 10522